Piece Work

*Norma,
Thank you
for reading
and enjoying my
family.*

C. Williams
11/2/13

Piece Work

*Fields and Dreams
from the Central Valley*

C Mariano

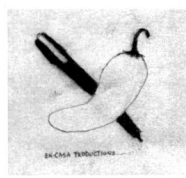

En-casa Production-cm

Piece Work
Copyright 2013 by Charles Mariano. All rights reserved. No part of this publication may be reproduced, stored in a retrieval system or transmitted in any form or by any means, electronic, mechanical, photocopying, digital recording or otherwise, without expressed written permission of the author.

Printed in USA
First edition published 2013

Cover design – ideas by design
'99' sign–Caltrafficsigns
Logo art – Laura Llano
Interior design and layout – ideas by design

Printing – MinuteMan Press

Library of Congress Cataloging-in-Publication Data
ISBN: 978-0-9910498-0-6

Table of Contents

FAHNS	1
Piecework	4
Sunday Morning in Merced	5
Unfinished Business	6
Fields & Dreams	8
Daddy's Skin	10
Driving Down The Santa Fe (1998)	14
Broken Home	17
Saving Gilbert	18
Tomato Planting in Merced	20
Ditchtender	21
Father's Day	25
In the Mix	26
Purple People Eater	32
Too Small to Burn	33
Alligator Hands	34
Toil & Sweat	35
Squatters	36
Heartland	37
Pruning Season	40
Sticking Tomatoes (1967)	42
Hotbeds	44
Magic Kingdom	50
SF Farmer's Market (Alemany)	53
Late Summer	54
Bus Stop	56
The Recorder (2008)	58
This Winter	59
Where Old Tractors Go To Die (Bright's in Le Grand)	61
The House on 12th	63
Footprints	64
Sunday Visit	66
Cactus House	68
Shoes	70
Tortillas and Bread	71
Tio Mike	72
The Artist (For Gilbert "Magu" Lujan)	73
The Snake Lady (2008)	74
Overplayed	78
Farming	80
Rearview	81
The 99	84
Benjamin Samuel	85
Alzheimer's (2005)	89
First Rain	90
Picture Books (2002)	92
The Reason For (2005)	94
The Family Place	95
Old Grey Suitcase	96
Plastic Flowers (2006)	98
Credits	104
Chicken Adobo	108
Pancit Recipe	109

Merced Arch, 16th street, circa 1920 (Merced County Historical Society Archives)

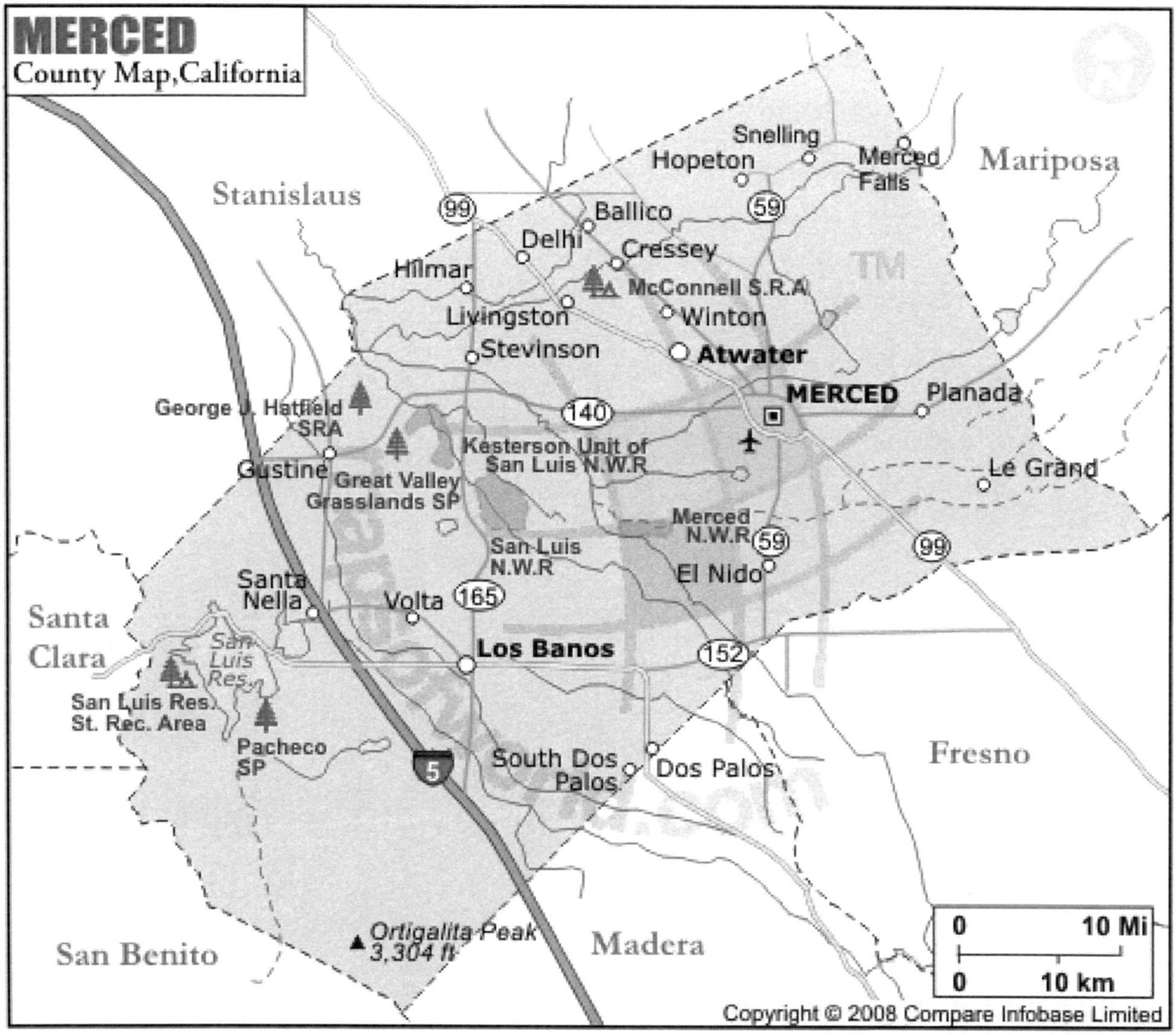

MERCED
County Map, California

15th Street, Sacramento, CA, circa 1950 (Caltrafficsigns)

"You were born to write this."

Marie Delgado Travis, December 19, 2012

For Daddy

Letter dated February 12th 2007, to Filipino American National Historical Society (Central Valley Chapter), later published 2008 in the FANHS book, "Talk Story"

FANHS,

Looking back on my life, especially the early years in Merced, always warms my heart, particularly when thinking of my father. Fond memories. I moved away from Merced over thirty years ago to attend UC Davis with intentions of returning, but settled down and stayed in Sacramento. Most of my family is still there, so the visits are mixed with emotional highs and lows, because I'm at an age where losing loved ones is becoming too familiar.

It was October 7, 2006, during one of many trips to the hospital in Merced to visit my ailing brother John, that my sister Dolores and I took a break from the stress and found the streets blocked off and teeming with activity. The event was the Big Valley Festival. Watching our brother suffering in that dismal room for months had completely drained us, so the people, booths,

Daddy with friend and bucket of tomatoes, circa 1950

and music, was a welcome sight. As Daddy would often say, "Just what the doctor ordered."

Since I've been gone, Merced has grown immensely. The hospital I was born in is no longer Merced General, and even 17th Street, "The Drag" as we knew it, is now called Main. We parked the car over on 18th and strolled through the various colorful booths near what used to be the Strand Theater. We bought something to eat and drink, then sat down on the curb to watch the cultural dancing in the middle of the street.

Just down the street from where we sat I spotted an interesting booth with big boards and lots of pictures. It was dozens of black and white photos of Merced Filipino history. I've always been fascinated by old pictures, so I took my time

Piece Work · 1 · Slices of Life

looking them over. This was indeed Merced Filipino history, but something was missing. I called Dolores over, and after searching through them, she thought the same thing I did. "Where's Daddy? Daddy should be on that board."

John Ramos Mariano, born in Isabella of the Philippine Islands in 1910, is as much a part of Filipino history in Merced as anyone on that board. I'm not exactly sure what year he came to town, but he met and married a beautiful Mexican girl named Mary Alonzo. By the time I was born, they'd been separated already, so I'd never seen them as husband and wife. No matter what house we were in though, they were always Mama and Daddy.

It was like being raised in two cultures. My favorite side, was my Filipino side. During most days we'd be in town at some rundown rental place at a dozen different locations. Daddy lived on Olive Avenue, which in those days was out in the sticks, in what seemed like a million miles in the country. He lived in a combo setting where half was a small kitchen and sleeping quarters attached to the back of a large wooden garage, and the other half was tiny trailer where he slept and two beds. The main house was owned by his cousin Nick Gauiran.

The other part of the living quarters for the bare necessities, was the outhouse about 50 yards down a hill. Many a scary night was spent going to that outhouse where every spider and snake imaginable lurked in the darkness. In the center of that combo was a tin shack used for bathing. It was a large square tub that was filled with a waterhose to a certain level. During winter nights we added big pots of boiling water to keep from freezing.

Behind the house we were surrounded by a grove of almond trees. Out front, running all along Olive Avenue, was a fast-moving canal where we swam day and night during summer. Facing Olive on our left were the rich white folks, the Kennedys, and immediately the opposite direction and across the street was the Balanon's house. Much further down Olive, closer to G street, were the Baladad's.

It never occurred to me how poor we were, or that other people looked down on us and treated us different. Daddy protected us from all that. In fact, this place with its swimming canal, bee boxes in the almond orchard, and countless trees, was a glorious place of adventure.

I realized later on how painfully ashamed Daddy felt of his poorness, especially to other Filipinos. It wasn't just being poor, it was the rumors behind his back. Rumors of "his" kids and that Mexican woman. He spent most of his life slaving in hot dusty fields during the day, and working as a janitor at Castle Air Force Base on graveyard shift. He always seemed dirty from working the fields, his skin hard, calloused, and burned. Despite his hard work, the relentless needs of us children, it was never enough.

Somehow Daddy endured and found that long sought respect late in life, through farming. We worked the fields with other Filipino farmers like Tony Dumpit, Primo Hullana, Mel Acosta, and many more. Pioneers in a small movement of farming pinoys growing and shipping tomatoes and other vegetables to the Farmers' Market in San Francisco.

I remember telling my brother last year that some days, I feel more Filipino than I do Mexican. "The best of both worlds," I told him. My brother John Jr., passed away three days after I visited Merced last October. Coincidentally, he appeared in the Merced Sun-Star obituary, side by side with friend and fellow classmate, Donald Madayag.

My father died March 26, 1979 at the age of 69. On the surface, he was never successful enough to be worth noting. That is, unless you go by the size of his heart. If you knew him, you truly loved him. There were no rewards, or trophies when he left us. His memory is preserved through his children and family pictures. In my mind, there was no greater sacrifice, than the life he gave us.

So it's my Filipino side writing to you today saying, John Ramos Mariano, former president of the Merced Tomato Growers, my mentor, my hero, the biggest man in town, rightfully deserves mentioning in Merced's Filipino history.

respectfully,

Charles Mariano

Piece Work

While walking to the library to attend a meeting a few months back, I stopped to scribble a poem that was in my head about working in the fields. I'd written a few things on this topic through the years, so this was just another. By the time I got to the front door, I finished the poem, scribbled the title, Piece Work, then went inside.

While sitting at a table of friends, not really listening, I thought about gathering up the few fieldwork poems I'd written, and making them into a small chapbook. Then I thought the title of the poem worked better as the title for a book.

I got back to the office and started digging around for those old poems. Found about six, but also found a few old stories and essays that might fit too. Then an image or photo came to mind. Before I knew it, ideas and pages kept coming until I was overwhelmed. Curiously, every time I found something that worked well, my father kept popping up in the lines, a common thread. I realized there's no way to write about fieldwork or farming without including him.

A couple of weeks later, it hit me, "Ohh I get it, this is a book about Daddy." After that, everything made sense.

My father, John Mariano died many years ago, so it was going to take some serious digging to reconnect. I'd forgotten much of it, or tried to, by keeping it in a safe place. I never admitted it at the time, but his loss hit me hard. It was a wound buried deep, that sooner or later, I was going to have to face.

The term Piece Work is familiar to anyone who's ever done field work. You either worked by the hour, or by contract, more commonly known as piecework. The term also works from a writing perspective, because that's what these pages are, writing pieces, slices of life growing up in my hometown. I don't live in Merced anymore, but most of my cherished memories are from there.

Daddy holding box of tomatoes, circa 1950

I would go back to the hot and dusty fields, swimming holes, fishing spots, and lively birthday parties, to tie all the pieces together. Eventually I'd hear and feel my father. This book could easily be titled, "Searching For My Father." I lost him one tragic day over thirty years ago, and now it's time to find him again. Little did I know, it was my father, who'd find me.

Finally, this is not a book about Filipinos, nor is it a book about Mexicans. It's a book about my father, my mother, my cultural family, and how hard we worked to survive in a small town in the Central Valley. No matter how many years, or how many miles away, I keep going home.
CM
2013

Sunday morning in Merced

*Exit to J Street,
now MLK (AARoads)*

it's not like
this town, this place
of youthful memories
is gone

it's just that
growing up here
looking back
through the years
it's become this distant
dreamlike quality

it pours
from every house,
every corner
young, beautiful faces
smiling, laughing

still here

not the solemn
hazy greys,
final emptiness

maybe it's the way
i dream,

warm, luxurious rivers
endless flows
holding, loving
never letting go

my own, personal
blindness

Grandma Socorro, Mama, cousin Natalia (front)

Unfinished Business

I was on the phone a while ago with my sister Dolores. Up to now I hadn't revealed much about what I was doing as far as putting together these latest pieces of my life…our life, by retracing Daddy's steps.

We started talking about my deceased brother's grandson, a victim of a shooting in Merced last week, another tragic loss. It was strange to see the same name as my brothers' printed in the headline of the Merced Sun-Star. I never knew this Benjamin even existed. When he was born, he disappeared into the many-layered folds of the city. "Did he look like Benjie?" I asked Dolores. "Yeah he did," she answered, "he was dark-skinned too, and recently had a baby." It troubled me, that I never met him.

Eventually we got around to discussing Christmas, which was a couple weeks away. Since Mama died, Thanksgiving and Christmas holidays are usually spent at my sister's house on V Street. She'd make the enchiladas, I'd bring pies from Costco, everybody pitched in.

I wanted to talk to her mostly about what I've been doing the last few weeks. Wanted to hear how it sounded out loud. "I'm putting something together about Daddy," I said. She paused a second, waited for me to fill-in the blanks. "It's funny," I told here, "I didn't know I was writing about Daddy until yesterday."

I'd done a book about my mother a few years ago, now I'm working on one for my father. He was such a loving influence in all our lives, especially for me. I've always felt a powerful bond with him.

Through the years, I've become sort of the family recorder, the one that takes the time to write things down. Don't know why, but I'm always taking notes. Scattered, seemingly unimportant pieces written decades back, that only now make sense. I read the pages, fragile threads of existence, complete with dates, and relive years, that would otherwise be forgotten.

I first wrote a few things about Daddy after he died, over thirty years ago. A difficult period of confusion, that cut deep, left me drained. I remember calling my brother Junie one night to verify some details, and could barely get the words out. He'd listen to me all shaken up, trying to recreate an incident over the phone. He called Dolores afterwards. "I'm worried about Charlie Boy writing about Daddy," he told her, "it's too

Daddy and my brothers with friends, circa 1960. Daddy, 3rd adult standing from left, Junie second from right, Benjie in front.

much for him, he can't take it." He was right at the time, so slowly, ever so gently, I set it aside, to give it more time.

"I've been doing research, retracing Daddy's footsteps," I told Dolores, "I started by reading his old letters." I had one of the letters in my hand as I told her this. I pressed my finger to the ink on the yellowed pages, his unmistakable handwriting, touched the address he wrote at the top of the page:
FOB Camacam, Santiago, Isabela, Feb. 13, 1979. My dearest Charlie Boy...

I read his words now, more than thirty years later, and can hear his soothing voice, feel him reaching across the ocean. I stop, notice my heart racing, take deep breaths to calm down.

"Last night I woke up from a sound sleep," I tell her, "with his words in my head. I got up, went to the living room to write. It's like he's talking to me, won't let me go back to sleep until I write it down."

My sister listens quietly, waits for me to catch myself, as if telling her this now, makes it officially real. She lets me go through the long, winding avenues of explanation, reconnecting, because she knows.

Dolores and I have always been close, a year apart, and in many ways, directly linked to Daddy. "He's with me now," I say to her, "We're working in the fields, driving to San Francisco to the Farmer's Market, he's playfully tossing me in the air, before getting ready for school. He's in this room, he's in all my rooms."

She listened quietly, waited through the obvious emotional pauses until I finished, then said, "It's been so many years. I wondered when you'd go back for Daddy. It's time."

Daddy

FIELDS AND DREAMS (Merced '66)

woke up, dressed
into work clothes
then crawled to the kitchen

Mama was up
rolling fresh torts
eggs con nopales,
packed
into a paper bag

walked to Food Center
on J street
to stand with others
wrapped, bundled, faceless
waiting for the bus,
any bus

they pulled to the curb
counted, loaded us
different fields
different crops

this time south
past LeGrand
just off the 99
a tomato field
tangled greens and reds
stretched across miles
of furrowed dirt

Funeral march 1994 for Cesar Chavez, Delano, CA (photo copyright Francisco Dominguez)

we arrived in darkness
just before light,
and for a few seconds
gazed in silence
as the sun rose
across the majestic grandness,
this holy ground
of sprawling green, deep red jewels
that rolled endlessly
towards the mountains of Mariposa
into the morning sun

bent, aching bodies,
stepped wearily into the rows
with dented, metal buckets
to fill the big trailers

soon,
an army of dark figures
bent silhouettes,
plunging, picking
pulling back vines,
a fast, rhythmic pace
scratched our skin raw,
turned our hands
dark green,

marched steadily
blindly
into the sun

Sign on 16th at Bear Creek Bridge, leaving Merced

DADDY'S SKIN

Most of my life, my father was always the darkest in the family. He worked in the fields so much, his skin burned to a leathery dark. He was always going to, or coming from, some backbreaking job in the fields. In those early years in Merced, scratching out a living was every day. You don't work, you don't eat.

My father passed away while I was in my first year of college at UC Davis over thirty years ago. It doesn't seem possible so much time has passed. Up to that point he was my number one reason for being in college. From grammar school on, I wanted to please him, make him proud. Daddy stressed school over all else, there was no other option.

My generation was born in California, and had all the required Americanizing we could handle, just not the income. Growing up, I liked The Lone Ranger, Leave it to Beaver, and Sky King. I played Gary Cooper dozens of times, walking bravely down that street in High Noon. Like him, I was the quiet hero who rises to the occasion to save the town, blazing away bad guys with my plastic six-guns.

When playing cowboys and Indians as a kid, I was shocked to learn Indians weren't all blood-thirsty savages trying to scalp white folk. Even more shocking, I could play the Indian parts. My wake-up call was seeing Jay Silverheels as Tonto in the Lone Ranger. Before that, I was always the masked guy never realizing my skin color put me closer to the Indians. It was like ripping off Kimosabe's mask and finding Tonto. Tonto was a different kind of Indian, smart and strong, and strangely enough, looked like one of my cousins.

Daddy and Mama never lived together in my

Daddy

lifetime, so we were Mexican-American, and Filipino households, which at the time was no big deal. For me it meant more places to explore and play. Two houses, two very hip cultures, but still very poor. The day we moved into the brown duplexes on K street, 'the projects,' we thought we'd hit the bigtime. Despite our dismal surroundings though, we were loved in both houses, and that's all that mattered.

As we got older, we worked in the fields a lot, but not like the migrant families that rolled in seasonally to work the crops. It's funny, but even they seemed to have more than we did. Bundled under layers of clothing, they were organized labor machines. Most spoke only Spanish, or had heavy accents, easily mistaken for ignorance. The ignorant ones out in the fields, was us, and we came in all colors.

I remember walking out in the early darkness to stand across from Food Center grocery store on J street to catch the bus to chop cotton, pick tomatoes or whatever. The Central Valley was abundant in all crops. The locals like me, worked summers, got a firsthand blistering of the hard life. We knew eventually we'd rejoin the city school system and let Daddy take on the burden of field work. Daddy worked the fields and orchards year round, pruning, prepping, planting, wherever the job or town was.

Eventually, Daddy leased small plots of land to farm, so we stopped catching the work bus, and went to our own field. Didn't make the work easier, in fact, it was harder, because there was more at stake. Daddy never let up though, preaching to me often, how this life wasn't going to be mine. His dream was for me to succeed through school. His dream, became my dream.

Pleasing Daddy in school gave me a great sense of pride. I loved to see his face light up whenever he got my report card. Even the smallest accomplishment made him happy. He made a point of setting aside time after dinner and television, no matter how exhausted he was, to teach me from books he collected or bought. We'd sit on the bed in his little trailer and go over page after page, until I was too sleepy. When school started, most of the stuff they taught, I already knew.

It would be nice to have a storybook ending, but that's not how life is. I got a phone call from my sister Dolores in Merced, while I was away in college, telling me Daddy died while in the Philippines. It stunned me. It seemed at the time, my life stopped cold. When I left Merced he was always with me, even when he wasn't. Now, suddenly I was alone.

I soon lost sight of personal health and responsibilities. I didn't pay bills, didn't eat, and didn't care. I didn't want to see anyone, so I shut the doors and windows, and sunk into denial. It's strange, but at the time I thought I was dying, and dying alone in my room, was better than dying in plain sight.

If there's a saving grace, it came from Daddy again. Always Daddy. This time, through long, emotional dreams. In one, Daddy's holding my hand, comforting, healing. We're sitting on the bed in his trailer, and he's explaining, teaching me again. After a while, I can sense that he wants me to go, and I don't want to. I beg him to let me stay, but he gives me a gentle, loving push, and sends me home. I'd wake up crying.

Recently, at a gathering with Filipinos, someone spoke up and said, "You don't look Filipino." For a moment, I took offense, but it's true. Because of my father, I didn't spend a lifetime working in the fields like him, so my skin isn't burned dark. It's more of a light tan. When my father died thirty years ago, it seemed, so did my Filipino side. Almost overnight, I became more Mexican. Still rich in culture, but missing a big piece.

I told the man at this gathering, the way I've addressed the question of skin color before, "It's ok," I told him, "John Mariano is definitely my father, and in fact, he's my hero. Besides, I've been told I don't look Mexican either."

Top left, Santana poster Merced Fair, 1969. Random pages 1939 Merced County Fair program.

Merced County Library: (Merced County Historical Society)

Piece Work | Slices of Life

Driving Down the Santa Fe (1998)

There was a road that my brother Junie and I drove the last time we went fishing the San Joaquin River, that brought back memories. After that fishing trip, we spent the night at cousin Ponchie's house in Turlock, and planned to hit the 99 back to Merced in the morning. We decided to take the back way home instead, down Santa Fe Road.

While driving that road, the landscape and scenery started looking familiar. It reminded me of things from a long time ago. "Did we come fishing out here as kids?" I asked Junie.

"That's Ballico," he answered, "We're headed right by it." He started rattling off all these places as we neared them, and other things we did when we were young. Places I'd forgotten.

(Caltrafficsigns)

Since I'm the only one in my family to leave town and attend college, it seems like I'm always gone. The years that passed in between flashed too quickly. When my brother Benjie died two years ago, Junie, my sister Dolores, and I were sitting outside Mama's house the night before the burial, stunned with disbelief. Losing Benjie at 44 was a brutal awakening.

I've always been close to my family, but the distance between Sacramento and Merced prevents me from being actively involved like the rest. It's a shame, really, because the distance isn't really that far. Less than a two hour drive north and south, on the 99. What was I doing that was so important? It's amazing what death does to your sense of priority.

That night, while the three of us sat outside drinking a beer, I made a silent promise to get closer, to find a way to give more time to my family. For the first time in my life, the phrase, 'Life's too short,' scared the hell out of me.

Junie and I hadn't been fishing in at least fifteen years. I went away to college, then again to another college, and in between, Junie married three times. My visits home were brief and spending very little time with him. I knew fishing was his great passion, because he talked about it constantly whenever I called, so I decided to set up a fishing trip and included my cousin Ponchie. I'd lost the fishing bug a couple decades back, dismissing it as a lazyman's sport. I was more into the physical side of exercise, but wanted to do this for my brother. It was time.

I remember that day I called long distance to tell him. "Junie, I want you to get things ready when I come home next week, because we're going fishing." He thought I was kidding, because fishing was his thing, not mine. "Junie, do you hear me? I'm coming home next week. Pack the gear, and have Mama cook up tacos to-go. We're going fishing."

It's hard to describe the feeling I got telling him, and how he felt hearing it. I'm not ashamed to admit the love and closeness between brothers that came from this. A closeness we'd lost somewhere in our busy lives, let slip away. This fishing trip was for him, and for me. He was my big brother again in charge of the gear, the vehicle, and where we were going.

The first fishing trip was, as my Dad used to say, a 'Kodak' moment. It was the most fun and satisfying time in many years, because it opened my eyes to everything I'd been missing. I had to stop for a moment to take it all in. It's really not about fish. I knew that, just needed a reminder. I needed to slow down, breathe deeply.

The most glorious surprise of all was that it reminded of times with Daddy. The worst pain I'd ever felt in my life was when Daddy died. I doubt I'll ever recover from that. But out there on the river, the smell of mint bushes, mosquitos and frogs, the sound of the reel winding, rewinding, brought him back to me. This is where my father is.

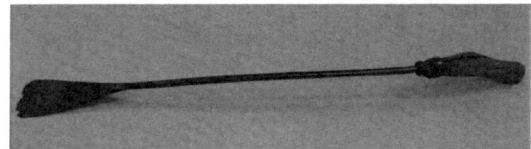

Asparagus knife (San Joaquin Historical Society, Lodi, CA)

Everything, it seems, happened just a short distance off the Santa Fe. In Winton, I remember the sweet potato and watermelon fields we worked and farmed about a mile or two from the road. I remember the day one of the black kids my age was run over by his father's truck when we were pitching melons just before dark.

I remember playing hooky from Merced High my freshman year, with friends, and driving to Winton to a swimming place just under Shaffer Bridge, near that same field where we worked. There was a big tree and rope swing. I could hear us yelling and laughing that day. I see Gilbert, my good friend, who couldn't swim, but jumped in anyway. I remember jumping in too late to save him, dragging him by his hair to the side out of the water, and freaked when he coughed, came back to life.

I think about that fishing trip with Junie and Ponchie last year, and the decision to drive home down the Santa Fe the day after, a stretch of road I hadn't been on in years. Everything about that road and all the stops in between involved growing up working in the fields, swimming, fishing, and living. For some reason, I stopped taking that road, choosing the faster, more convenient, Highway 99.

There were miles of orchards, trees, fishing spots out there. It seems we farmed every acre of land up and down the road. Further down from Winton was a hole-in-the-wall town called Ballico. There was a narrow, winding road that went down to another bridge, then across it, where Daddy cut asparagus every summer.

Shaffer Bridge Winton, CA (photo Jasmin Mariano)

Daddy used a knife about two feet long, with a sharp flat end, to cut deep into the peat sand to the white stem of the asparagus. The handle was a crude wrapping of cloth and tape, that fit like an old pistol handle. To this day, I consider cutting asparagus in that bent over position, in desert-like conditions, the hardest fieldwork job ever, and I've worked a few. Only Filipinos worked in the asparagus. Only Filipinos of my father's generation.

About a quarter mile from that asparagus field in Ballico, the outer edges of the river, were thick rows of plum trees that lined the lush area along the bank. When we climbed up the small hill and walked down to the river, it was like coming out of the desert and stepping into a hidden paradise.

Daddy brought us here to go fishing and swimming. I remember the day my brother Benjie fell off the bridge and almost drowned when he was six. And the day Daddy carried me to the deep part of the river to teach me to swim. He's holding me by my belly, just above the water. "Kick Charlie Boy, kick."

Merced River (photo courtesy of Mike Osborn, Friends of the River)

On the other side of that river, the water trickled off to a gully during off-season, and separated from the main body into a dead stream. Daddy gave us buckets and rubber boots, and we waded into the mud to dig for clams. And after the rains, we'd go back to that same area, where Daddy cut giant hongos (mushrooms) from the bottom of the trees, which Mama cooked with meat and white rice.

Driving down the Santa Fe that day was like driving the Route 66 of my childhood. I know it's just a road, but like the 99 that connects us north to south, it's the mighty Merced River flowing down from the mountains of Yosemite into the Central Valley, that become all our rivers, living pieces, that make this home.

As we drive away, the rivers, fields, and Daddy, slowly fade from my back window and melts dreamily into my heart.

Merced River (photo courtesy of Mike Osborn, Friends of the River)

Broken Home

every night
after a long day
of working the fields
Daddy came to us
without fail

his skin
caked hard from the sun
eyes burnt
to a squint

his old pick-up
a patchwork
of blue, orange, and rust,
barely drivable

the door creaked
as he stepped down
stomped the pavement
to knock the dust,
then used a wet rag
to wipe a clean spot
on his face

stooped shoulders
dusty felt hat
his body
exhausted, beaten

by the time
he reached the torn screen door
he'd be smiling
scooping, kissing us
one by one

every day
through the window
i waited
for his old pick-up
ached for him

Me, 3-years old

SAVING GILBERT

when i was fourteen
a freshman at Merced High,
and on the way to school one day
my friend says,

"let's ditch, go swimming"
it was a hot day,
so we did

Gilbert Musquiz
sang for the Soul Flames,
a popular band in town
and from the get-go
all style and flash

i was...
well i was nobody

we met two other friends
from the band,
and drove from Merced
to Winton, at Shaffer Bridge,
where there was a ropeswing

despite the hot day
it was spring runoff
the river was ice cold

all through high school
i never smoked, or drank
everyone else did
Stonecold Sober,
was almost my nickname

on the drive there
they grabbed some alcohol
and drank to be drunk
by the time we hit the water,
they were

eventually we were all swinging,
dropping into the freezing water

Gilbert, bragged constantly
about his swimming exploits
all the way there,
and still hadn't gone in,
so i turned back to him
and yelled,

"hey Gilbert, quit talkin
and jump in!"

he got up all cool and smooth
grabbed the rope,
went back a few extra steps
then cut loose a mighty swing
"good one Gilbert!" i yelled

then he let go

i stared at the spot where he dropped,
a long time, too long,

he popped up briefly,
arms flailing,
then disappeared

that's when it hit me,
"he can't swim!"

i yelled at the guys far downstream,
waving my arms frantically
"Gilbert's drowning!"

all they had to do was wade out a little,
and he'd come right to them,
but they just stood there dazed,
and watched
as he bobbed near them,
then went by

i realized then, they were too drunk
and Gilbert had drowned,

it was a long way to him,
but dove in anyway, thinking
too late to save him
but had to get his body,
keep it from going miles downriver

took me awhile to get to
a shallow spot,
where i guessed he might be

i looked down into the clear water
a few seconds, and there he was,
staring up
with dead, bugged-out eyes,
scared the hell out of me

i screamed, closed my eyes
then reached down,
grabbed him by his hair,
started kicking, working my way
to the bank

i dragged him up on it
and instinctively,
flipped him over, like i saw on tv,
saying over and over,
"Gilbert's dead. Gilbert's dead"

then he jerked hard,
and started coughing up water

i stared at him in disbelief,
"you're alive!"
i dropped to the ground
shaking, crying

they said i saved his life,
kept telling them,
"no, i wasn't saving him,"
but they weren't buying it

could never figure why
he let go of the rope,
knowing he couldn't swim
all that big talk, almost killed him

word got back to Gilbert's mom
who grabbed me first chance,
and squeezed so tight,
i almost passed out

Shaffer Bridge, Winton, CA (photo by Paul Martzen)

Tomato Planting in Merced

in a conversation with Chuck,
gentleman and guardian
of a table and post
at McHenry Museum in Modesto
yesterday,

amid displays
of ancient tools
rusted, dug and preserved
from Central Valley farming
of days gone by,

i'm reminded of planting season,
in the hot, dusty fields
just off the Los Banos Highway
in Merced

of an old watertank planter
pulled by a small ford tractor
with two bent metal seats
in back, low to the ground

the water spout
between my father and I,
points down
into the dry, thirsty dirt

Daddy and I,
take turns
dropping Ace tomato plants
into the furrowed groove
six inches apart

each of us
with a lug of plants
in our lap
nurtured from seed
in the old glassframed hotbeds,
back of the house on Cone Avenue
during winter

Working on the Planter (courtesy Busa Farms)

as we chugged
across the field
under the blazing sun

i yelled to my brother
driving tractor up front,

"Junie! runnin low on water!"

he looks back, then up at the sun
to see how much daylight left,
his face ringed with dust and sweat
nods his head, then turns
at the end of the next row
to head back to the canal
to restart the pump

DITCHTENDER

beneath the blazing
Central Valley sun
my sunburnt legs stretched,
sprawled
over a soft dirt mound,
feet in the water

i hear a whistle
in the distance
stand, shield my eyes
see Daddy
waving his shovel
handle up, side to side

i signal back
with my shovel

my job,
watch for water breaks,
this side of the field

every year
we lease small patches of land
nomad farmers,
borrowed dirt
this time,
just off the Santa Fe tracks
near Winton

endless furrows
of sweet potato plants
yams

every few spaces
curly plastic pipes
lined up like soldiers
snaked over small ditches dug
to get the canal water
to the plants

Daddy whistles again
waves his shovel,
this time, scoop side up

'big break'

i grab my boots
my shovel,
and hotstep to other side

Planting fig cuttings in LeGrand, circa 1927
(Merced County Historical Society Archives)

Laborers (Busa Farms)

Tomato Picki[ng] 1947

g Crew

San Joaquin County Historical Society, Lodi, CA

Top:
Working asparagus sled (San Joaquin Historical Society, Lodi, CA)
Below:
Mexican laborers arriving train station Stockton, CA, circa 1950
(Russell Lee, Library of Congress)

Father's Day

it's strange, how every year
like clockwork
i come to this blank page
to remember my father

strange, because he never really left

every year
i set aside
a quiet moment
for us, only us

more than thirty years ago,
still hurts
wish it could've been different

"i know you're not coming back!"
i yelled angrily into the phone

refused to go to the airport
no goodbye, nothing

should've gone
should've hugged you,
told you i loved you,
held tight

stupid, stupid son
when they called
to tell me you died
walled myself away
every raw, agonizing cry
killed me, just killed me
until i healed,
or thought i did

you were everything Daddy,
all mine, everything
never should've left,
never…

every year, my father

Daddy and Mama with baby Junie, circa 1949
Applegate Park, Merced, CA

In The Mix

Don't know why I bother to write this, because there must be thousands of mixed Mexican/Filipinos in this world. What difference is one voice? I suppose since my father's been gone for over thirty years now, that his time on earth is not even worth noting. Then again, I know better. All I have to do is sit still for a moment, and he comes home to me.

John Ramos Mariano came to the United States from the Philippine Islands to find fame and fortune. He ended up in Merced, California, by way of Stockton, working in the hot fields of the Central Valley. Details fail me now, but somehow he managed his way to Kansas, attended college there, then returned to Stockton working in the fields. The reason he came back is vague, but he landed in Merced, a small town just up the 99, from Stockton.

Daddy with friends, circa 1950

I was a middle child and very young, so my older brothers understood his background better, and unfortunately they've both passed away. For me, it was as if all that time before he drove into the Merced city limits, didn't count. He met a lovely Mexican girl named Mary Alonzo, and eventually their six children, and my life, began from that point on.

Since very young, I was always in awe of my father. He wasn't big, imposing, or rich. In fact, there wasn't anything about him worth noting, but somehow he stood out. It's strange too, looking at pictures of him now, to see him slim and vibrant with a full head of hair. From the first moment I could appreciate his loving touch, comprehend his warm smiling face, he seemed already older. It was as if I was cruelly excluded from participating the first half of his life.

My father was deceptive in appearance. He was only about 5' 6," with a slightly rounded body, and very little hair on his head. He had dark, thick-calloused skin from working in the sun every day. Daddy was always in the fields, and always dusty and dirty. To me though, he was like a quiet superhero in disguise. Underneath that disheveled, sunburnt exterior was someone much bigger.

Daddy had a friendly smile, with eyes that twinkled happily when he spoke. When meeting strangers, particularly white people who at first glance dismissed him for his ragged appearance, he would surprise them with excellent English without a hint of accent, and with knowledgeable, witty conversation. He also spoke Filipino and flawless Spanish. It wasn't just that though; if you were around him, even for a little while, you knew, he was a genuinely sincere, good man.

"What town were you born in Daddy?" I asked when I was about eight years old. "Isabela, in the Philippines," he answered. It sounded wildly exotic and faraway. He reached down to hold my hands, and I'd be amazed every time, at how cracked and scaly they were from working in the fields. "You have alligator hands Daddy," I told him. He laughed. They were so rough and damaged, it hurt to look. I held them with my small hands, rubbed them gently, tried to soothe the pains away. We lived a poor, but split existence in Merced. By the time I knew, or cared to understand, there were always two houses. Mama's house in town, and Daddy's shack out in the country on Olive Avenue. No matter what was going on, I preferred living with Daddy. I'd kick and scream to go with him every day. With Mama, it was the full Mexican culture with celebrations and music, right down to a constant diet of beans and tortillas. Even religion was split. Mama had me baptized Catholic as a baby, and Daddy had me baptized Pentecostal at fifteen. It was a baptismal of choice, complete with the Holy Ghost, or what I thought at the time was the Holy Ghost. I wanted it mostly to please Daddy. Anything to be closer.

Most of my friends and family were Mexican, because during the school year, I had to stay in town near everybody, plus, there were lots of relatives. When weekends came, I hurriedly staked my claim to go with Daddy, always fighting with my brothers for the honor. Going with Daddy to the country was an adventure. The place we stayed was a rundown shack and small trailer combo, but the surrounding property owned by the Gauiran's was an almond orchard, with a canal out front that became our swimming hole ten times a day in summer.

When we were with Daddy, it was the unique language and flavor of a different culture. White rice with every meal, instead of tortillas. The people around us spoke Filipino, or pigeon-English, always fun. It was also the unforgettable excitement of pig feeds, where the pig is shot, then hung upside down to drain every drop of blood into a large pan. The blood was cooked with vinegar and spices, whipped into a dark creaminess, then mixed with fried pork. This succulent dish I called chocolate meat makes my mouth water. We were the luckiest family ever. The best of both worlds.

Even when Daddy cleaned up, it was mostly clothes from the secondhand store. "The willy-willy," he used to call them. Besides not really being able to afford new things, he hated wasting hard-earned money. Sometimes he'd walk out of the willy-willy with a full suit, two pairs of shoes, three dress shirts, belts and socks, and spend less than ten dollars. He would beam with delight like he'd robbed them and gotten away with it. "Now we have money left to buy donuts," he smiled. He'd point the old Chevy home, and break into one of his made up songs along the way. We'd all join in, swinging and singing loudly, "Chik Koree Chik, Chilaki Chilak, Aunt Jemimah, Kookala Boomba!!" As soon as we got to the "Boomba" part, he'd reach over and tickle us.

When I grew older and worked side by side in the fields with Daddy, I became more and more curious of his other life, the one before us. Why would someone as hardworking, and obviously educated as he, be working in the fields? What put him in this place with us?

He was always coming in before light from his nightwatchman job at Castle Air Force Base to wake us up, then feed and send us off to school, before trudging off to the fields. There was a lot that was unspoken, accepted as routine in our house. All my life, he never held my mother affectionately, never shared intimacy. I'm sure he did before, but I never saw it. I could see the pain in his eyes in those early morning hours, as he glanced at the closed door of my mother's room. Inside with her, a different man. But he never confronted, wouldn't raise his voice. Daddy just looked away. I really believe all the time and affection in his world was transferred directly to us, and we never let up, drained every ounce. No matter how I shook it, it always pointed to my mother. His greatest love, his most magnificent failure. She broke his heart, practically killed him. We kept him alive.

When it came to Parent/Teacher Conferences, Mama never attended. Mama was rarely home in those days, and felt intimidated, because she couldn't read and write. Daddy would come to every meeting, every event, straight from the fields, tired and caked in dust. The only clean parts on him was the feeble attempt to wash his hands and face. Mrs. Myers, my teacher in fifth grade Galen Clark Elementary, ended class early for Parent/Teacher night and had those students with parents scheduled early, wait behind. I dreaded Parent/Teacher days. Daddy would come, and definitely dirty. Everyone would see him.

I faked an excuse to go to the bathroom and went outside to check the parking lot. Sure enough, there he was coming out that clunky old pickup, stomping his boots hard on the pavement to knock off the dirt. Patty Gomez walked by and said, "Isn't that your father coming down the hall?" I looked away angrily and said, "That ain't my father! I don't know who

Galen Clark Elementary 1962, Mrs. Meyers 5th grade class

Old pick-up, Merced County (photo Emilio Soltero)

he is!" I went into the bathroom and stayed there a long time. I watched as Daddy and Mrs. Meyers finally came outside to the steps. She was talking, smiling, shaking his hand. How could I ever face her or the other classmates? Daddy looked around searching front and back, but didn't see me. I slid to the back of the fence, climbed over, and ran the five blocks home.

I didn't want to face Mrs. Meyers the next day, but had no choice. To my surprise, she took me aside and raved about Daddy. "Your father is the kindest, most charming man I have ever met. The fact that he came directly from the hot fields to take part in our Parent/Teacher meeting, tells me he is an extraordinary father." I expected to be punished, and instead was filled with a great sense of pride. One other thing I felt, was strangely ashamed. It was like that with every teacher, every conference. No matter how he looked, whenever they met him, they absolutely fell in love with him. They knew what I couldn't see at the time.

It takes a while for kids to see clearly, learn to appreciate. You wake up one day, let it roll through your sleepy eyes, and suddenly there's tears. I'd remember his rough hands. Those loving, alligator hands. Scene after scene of total pain and sacrifice unfolds. He lived through, and inside us. "Daddy, why aren't you a great success? Why did you stay with her? Why did you let us siphon every dime, every breath?"

Finally, the most painful point of all, the vicious rumor that he might not be our father. It just wasn't possible. There were whispers. Plenty of whispers from those, supposedly in the know, but we never let them get close to the wall of love and loyalty we'd built. I am the middle child of six. With each new birth, Daddy waited outside, gathered us in, gave us his name. He never blinked when it came to raising us. We were his children, no matter what anyone said. To this day, every one of us will fight to the death if you dare say otherwise.

"Are you Mexican, or Filipino?" someone asked. I could hear Daddy singing in my ear, "Chik Koree Chik, Chilaki Chilak, Aunt Jemimah, Kookala Boomba!!"

"I am the best of both worlds."

Standing in back: Tio Frank, Aunt Ruby, Mama, Daddy, cousin Natalia (front left)

17th Street/Main Merced, CA, circa 1955 (Merced County Historical Society Archives)

Purple People Eater

as a small boy
i have
flickering images,
fragments
that don't connect
completely,

of a house in Winton,
a tiny town near Atwater
next to
the Santa Fe tracks

we lived
in the country
near a river
there was a strong odor
of an onion plant
just beyond the orchards

i remember
chili juice on my left thumb,
Mama put
to keep me from sucking
and a tire swing
out back
that my brother pushed
higher and higher
until the rope broke,
along with my leg
most of all
i remember this crazy song
that played on the radio
same time
every morning,

Mama and i sang it
as i tied my shoes,

"It had one big eye, and two big teeth...
It was a one-eyed, one horned,
flying purple people eater..."

Galen Clark Elementary grades 4&5, 1961

Too Small to Burn

woke up,
stretched, unfolded
in the back seat

it's daylight,
already sweating

pulled myself up
to the window
squinting, searching
for Daddy and the rest,
bundled, tiny dots
far down the rows
of desert sand

"you're still too small,
and the job's, too hard,"
Daddy told me
in the morning darkness

like always,
i pleaded, cried
clung to his pants leg

he shook his head
wrapped me in his coat
then laid me in the back seat,
"you'll be sorry, it's hot out there"

cutting 'sparagus
somewhere in Ballico
by the bridge,
where we catfished
and swam
no trees
a sizzling, brutal sun

opened the door,
slipped down to the cool shade
of the big tire,
and waited anxiously,
for Daddy
to work his way back to me

Filipino workers cutting asparagus (Stockton Chapter, Filipino American National Historical Society)

Alligator Hands

most of the day we'd run barefoot and screaming
through the streets
climbing trees, fences,
breaking windows

we lived on 12th
one block
from the back fence
to the Merced Fairgrounds

climbed that fence
a hundred times
tore my pants twice

remembered sliding down
the giant sand pile
on flattened cardboards
when the workers left,
that became highway 99
the most thrilling time
every day,
was when Daddy came home
from working the fields

he climbed off
that rusty old pickup
stomped the dust and dirt
off his shoes,
wipe his eyes
with his shirtsleeve,
then bend down and scoop me up

it's his hands,
i remembered most
sunburnt black,
hard, and cracked

"alligator hands,"
i told him

he just laughed

Toil and Sweat

"stop shaking Charlie Boy, almost there...almost there"

it was about fieldwork
youthful growing years
in Merced,

about working
under that fierce
Central Valley sun
terrible, suffocating heat
that rose from the ground
like spiraling steam
where we wilted, didn't break

it was about working
by the box, or the pound,
straddling
a hundred miles
of furrowed dirt, bent
low to the ground
for speed
with that god-forsaken short hoe,
until my body screamed

it was about pieces
two loving cultures
cracked, blistered,
scraped raw

it was about twisted,
gnarled hands
too ravaged to pick
one more box,
and doing it anyway

mostly,
it was about working
side by side, with Daddy
protecting, reassuring, soothing,
filling my head
with impossible dreams
and a promise, to not let me die
in these fields,
like him

SQUATTERS

At the end of each season, Daddy scouted fields for next year's crop. Unused patches of land that he eyeballed from the road. Eventually he'd walk up to the owners, make the pitch to lease, but ask permission to check the soil. He'd walk from one to the other, pick up dirt clods, open them, crumble it through his fingers, smell it. "The dirt isn't ours, we just borrow it," Daddy explained.

Every year it was a different plot of land on the outskirts of Merced. There was never a successful harvest, only enough to break even, or worse. Still, Daddy was convinced the next year would be better. He'd save a little from the last crop, a handful of cash, and a sincere promise.

My brothers and I, looked at the field of ending crop, sadly. Tomatoes, bell peppers, and squash, wilted, dried yellow, flattened across the property, acres of carcasses. "Clean it up, put the dirt back like we found it," Daddy told us. After the plowing, we'd pack all the sticks, shovels, hoes, wire, pipes and boxes and haul it out.

The next day we drove to another side of Merced County, this time just outside Winton, to grow sweet potatoes. "Yams," Daddy called them. He'd partnered with a grizzly Mennonite with fiery red hair, named Archie Pister. I watched my brother Junie drive the rickety tractor through the gate to cultivate the ground for next year.

Daddy worked ten times harder than all of us. I marveled at his strength and endurance. He'd leave in the dark, come home in the dark. His body sloped, his skin burned so bad, he looked black, but always smiled wide through his aches.

He loved farming, even this dirt-poor, squatter's style that brought little reward and great pains. A bad harvest never broke his spirit, he'd just find another piece of land and start over.

There was something magical out there for Daddy, that took years for me to understand and appreciate. Why he kept going back, slaving under that unforgiving sun, working himself to death. It was there though, in his dirty, sweat-stained clothes, sacrifice, agony, overwhelming sense of pride. It was in his face before the first bit of dirt was turned. From seeds to sprouts, to plants, to first harvest bursting through soil in dazzling reds, greens, and yellow. It was with in his hands, it was in his heart.

One overcast day, just before heading into summer, he walked down the long line of planted furrows, then squatted low. "Here, come look," he coaxed, "these are okra." He waved his arm high and across to the left, "over there, jalapenos, bells, and watermelons." I kneeled, gently held the young plant in my fingers, and gazed out at the rows of green that went on forever. He smiled proudly, then kissed the top of my head, "Looks like a good year, Charlie Boy."

Sorting sweet potatoes, Merced County (Merced County Historical Society Archives)

Heartland

 i realize
after decades away
thousands of trips home,

Highway 99,
that stretch of road
between Sacramento and Merced,
is now part of me
and constant

holidays, family events
numbing, traumatizing
funerals,

on the 99, always the 99,

i realize
the winding rivers of my youth
flowing all directions
in Merced County,
are also constant

like the river
by Henderson Park
family gatherings,
rafting

or the river in Winton,
by Shaffer Bridge
where we swam,
just down the road
from the sweet potato fields,
we worked

and further down
in Ballico,
another bridge,
the river
where we catfished,
went swimming
near the asparagus fields,
where Daddy worked

Merced River (photo Mike Osborn, Friends of the River)

and later, as a teenager
drinking, driving
the backroads through Snelling,
along the river,
that led to Mariposa,
and higher,
all the way to Yosemite

from there
the powerful, mesmerizing
Merced River
that rages down the mountains
from Yosemite,
caressing rocks, boulders
to glistening jewels,

flowing wildly, mightily
to the lower valley,
that feeds
into all the streams and rivers
of my childhood

i realize now,
it's always been,

the Merced River
and the 99,

that binds,
connects,
converges,

takes me home

Background image- Grapes to prune, Lodi, CA
Insert image- Man pruning grapes, Stockton, CA (San Joaquin County Historical Society, Lodi, CA)

Pruning Season

I used to beg my father to let me go with him, whether in the desert-like heat of the asparagus fields in summer, or pruning trees and grape vines on freezing mornings in winter. I remember the air was so cold one morning, my breath made clouds of smoke. I was about six years old, still too small to help, but always insisted on going. I'd do anything just to be with Daddy.

During pruning season, Daddy would get jobs in Merced, and all around the central valley. This particular job was a peach orchard conveniently located across the street and owned by one of the neighbors down the road. We stayed in a little shack attached behind Nick Gauiran's garage on Olive Avenue. It was a combo set-up. The stove and sink was inside the shack, about ten feet from there was a small tin-roofed tub area for bathing, and another ten feet was the outhouse. The outhouse was the subject of many frightening experiences growing up, especially at night.

Daddy grabbed the ladders and we walked across the street with my older brother Junie to prune the trees. When we got there, the sun hadn't burned off the freeze yet, so the cold made my teeth chatter. I could see icicles on tree branches and the ground. My dad and older brother Junie built a small campfire in a clearing away from the trees to warm my hands.

After they got the fire going, Daddy and Junie carried their ladders further into the orchard where they left off the previous day, while I stayed behind by the campfire. It was so cold I had to stand close to the fire to keep warm. I'd talk to them while they worked up in the trees, by yelling, holding my hands over the fire.

Pruning apricots, Stockton, CA (San Joaquin County Historical Society, Lodi, CA)

Before I knew it, I felt a stinging on my leg and realized my pants caught fire. It was full flame before I noticed, and started screaming for Daddy to come help me. He flew down the ladder, raced through the rows of trees to me. By the time he got there, my whole right pants leg was on fire. Daddy threw himself on my legs in a full embrace, then rolled me over on the icy ground to douse the flames, then swooped me up in his arms and raced across the street into the car and to Merced General. I screamed and cried a lot, but lived.

On the drive back home, I apologized over and over to Daddy, because I knew they missed work, and we desperately needed the money. Daddy just looked over at me and smiled warmly, "Don't worry Charlie Boy, we'll work extra tomorrow."

The skin on my right leg was burned badly, a huge raw spot that got smaller through the years. Some of the hair on my leg grew around it, so it's hardly noticeable unless I point it out to somebody. When I wear pants, or regular socks, can't even see it.

Daddy's been gone a long time now. Once and awhile, I'll reach to the bottom of my right pants leg, pull it up a few inches to the burn spot, rub it gently, and smile. It's like touching Daddy.

Sticking Tomatoes (1967)

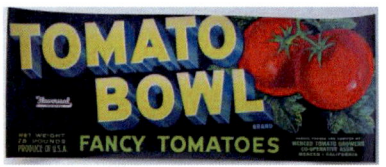

as we inched into another day
of summer heat,
Daddy rousted us
one by one
before light

we loaded up the flatbed
with more bundles
of long wooden sticks
sharp on one end,
flat on the other

the morning sun
peeked over the hood
of our battered truck

"Hurry up boys," Daddy yelled from the door
"hot one today"

at the field
a leased 10-acre spread
on Gerard Avenue in Merced,
we dropped the bundles
at the end of each row
of sprawling tomato plants

Jimmy Boy and Daddy
opened each bundle
and dropped one stick
every few feet
next to the plants

we used a large, hollow metal pipe
closed on one end,
with welded handles on the sides,
for pounding

we'd place each stick in the ground
by hand
then reach up and over
with the metal pounder,
slide it down to the end
and pound, gently at first
then harder
until the point
stuck firmly into the ground

after hours of pounding
hands calloused
arms and shoulders
aching,
we stopped
to catch our breath
and gazed ahead
at the hundreds of sticks,
yet to go

after the sticks pounded in
we hung large spools of twine
to our belts
and started stringing,

first one side, then the other
pulling each vine up, under the twine,
then looping it around
each stick

by the end of the week
the plants on the ground
all raised,
standing tall
soon,
a dazzling red harvest,
glistening jewels
held up, and out
just drag our lugs
between the rows,

easy pickins

Old tractor, Bright's Museum LeGrand, CA

HOTBEDS

Hotbeds (Busa Farms)

It's almost misleading to say we were farmers, because we weren't a real farm with mega-acreage, or with goats and chickens. We didn't even have a barn. We farmed, but didn't own the land, we leased it. If someone saw us, we'd look like a scene out of the Grapes of Wrath movie, only we weren't Okies, we were dark-skinned faces, firmly rooted in the Central Valley soil.

Growing the big garden was Daddy's thing. My brothers and I helped out when needed, but no matter how much we did, no one put in more hours, worked harder, than Daddy. His work didn't stop either, like it did for us during winter when we went back to school. He worked year round in fields and orchards all over Merced County and points beyond, preparing crops or orchards, pruning trees, tying grape vines, prepping the ground. In summer, it became backbreaking sweat from sunup to sundown.

One day Daddy decided he wanted to try his hand at growing his own, rather than working for someone else. He wanted to grow a big produce garden like the Filipino families we knew in town. We'd go visit the Filipino farmers out on Gerard Avenue and marvel at their efficient operation. Nice houses, new equipment, and big, strong sons and daughters. They never treated us badly, always welcoming us, but we felt like the wide-eyed, peon cousins. Daddy wanted what they had, a successful farming operation. Never mind that he didn't have a green thumb, and that it would take many failed years before getting it right, he was bound and determined. This was his calling. In that sense, it became ours.

We'd always work in the fields around Merced in summer to get extra cash for school clothes, or for the Merced Fair in June, but nothing like the farmworker families that came in seasonally from Mexico. Those people were on an organized mission. We were just random armies huddled on the sidewalk with the rest of the ragtag desperados, waiting for the work buses. By the time I was old enough to carry a bucket or swing a hoe, I was chopping, picking, pruning everything. If it grew out of the ground, sooner or later, we worked it.

When Daddy got the growing bug, it changed the way we did farm labor. There was no more piece work, or working by the hour. It was working with Daddy, side by side with my brothers, as a family. There was always plenty to eat, tomatoes, bell peppers, watermelons, sweet potatoes, straight out of the ground. We never got rich, but there was a great sense of pride now. This field, this food, and the hard work and sweat it took to make it, was ours.

Before any planting reached the fields, there were the hotbeds to tend to. That was the seedling-to-plant nurturing during winter, before transplanting to the big field, a critical part of

Hotbed frames stacked next to old truck (Busa Farms)

the growing process. I remember first seeing the hotbeds in the back yard of the house on Cone Avenue, two streets past Calvary Cemetery, near the Los Banos Highway. The house itself was an ugly, rundown square box with a flat roof, that looked like it was slapped together with scrap wood and cardboard, then painted over in patchwork brown. The first time I laid eyes on it, I thought, 'This place should be condemned.'

It was the backyard though, that Daddy was sold on. It was basically the neighborhood dumping ground with overgrown weeds. I saw a junkyard, Daddy saw hotbeds. He needed space to set them up, and the house on Cone had it. It took days to clean out the area in back, before Daddy started forming the hotbed layout. He set two long rows of side boards on each side, pounded them down, then firmed those up with stakes. I looked at it curiously, then looked up at my father. "This is where the plants are going," he told me. I still couldn't see it. The side boards had to be a precise distance across each row, because we had to lay about twenty big frames, end to end, all the way down. The best way to describe these frames, would be that they looked like large old-fashioned window frames. These were laid flat across the side boards, covering every open area in the middle. This was to protect the plants during winter, and reflect optimal light when the weather was good.

Daddy carefully planted seedlings into the hotbeds, according to his bible, The Farmer's Almanac. Once the seeds and plants were carefully planted inside the hotbeds, they were cared for like babies. At night, we had to unroll big canvas covers across the hotbeds to protect them on freeze nights. Daddy monitored weather reports like a hawk. In the mornings, we'd roll up the canvas, prop a small stick under every other frame to let the air and light in. On heavy rain days, we'd spread weighted plastic sheets across the frames.

As the plants got bigger, longer sticks were needed to give more space to grow, or until they were mature enough to transplant to the big field, which was a leased patch of land somewhere around Merced County, always a

House on Cone Avenue, Merced, CA

different place. It was common knowledge among the Filipino farmers, not to farm the same produce year after year on the same ground. So Daddy was out scouting long before summer, sometimes the year before, negotiating a deal with a local farmer to lease eight to ten acres of their land to plant our big garden.

By the time I was eighteen, and during my first year at Merced College, in a very…experimental phase of growing up, I tried smoking marijuana. That particular winter I ran across some really strong weed in town, one was called Panama Red, and the other Acapulco Gold. In those early days, even though everyone was doing it, the laws about smoking and possession were scary. After I'd finished my stash, I'm not sure why I thought it might be cool to save the seeds from the Acapulco Gold. So I put a few seeds into an old sock, then hid it in a drawer.

In those days I was very naïve and extremely paranoid about the seeds I'd saved. I was afraid Daddy would find them, and me, the 'supposed' good son with the brains to know better. The longer I thought about it, the more it freaked me out. I imagined the police finding the seeds and me going to prison. So one day I grabbed the old sock and sneaked out the back door to the furthest end of the backyard to hide them. Without really thinking about it too much, I lifted the frame of the hotbeds, sunk the seeds deep into the moist soil, then forgot about them.

About a month or so later, when we were alone, Daddy called me to the living room where he was watching television. "You need to get those things out of my hotbeds," he said to me point blank. I didn't have a clue what he was talking about, then it hit me, and my whole face and mind just crumpled into pathetic blubbering.

"Wha…wha..what things?" I answered, not really wanting to hear the answer.

I have no idea how he found out it was me who did this, but suspected my brother Jimmy ratted on me. "Charlie Boy, take those plants out of the hotbeds before we get in trouble," he insisted again. I knew it was useless to deny, it was right there in my deer-in-the-headlights face. What bothered me more than anything else, was I felt I'd let Daddy down. For most of my life, I was the one he had high hopes for, the one that was going to do something with my education, make him proud. All I could do now was hang my head in shame.

The strange thing about all this was the way Daddy told me, the tone of his voice, the expression on his face. He wasn't angry, didn't even look disappointed. He seemed almost amused. "Whatever those things are," he said, trying to keep a straight face, "take it out of the hotbeds. Its pushing the glass over." That part didn't register right away.

"What? I mean, yes, ok." I walked out of the room and raced out the back door.

Daddy had the glass frames propped to the highest possible point without tipping over. There they were, three huge plants, with stems that looked like small tree trunks. I was shocked to see this thing fully grown. I never imagined they could get this big. They looked like they were on steroids. Then I thought about how much time and nurturing Daddy puts into the hotbeds for the all the plants, feeding the soil, watering, raising the glass every day, covering at night. During the early growth stages, these mysterious baby plants grew firm and strong and just kept growing.

I got close to these monster plants, braced my feet across and pulled a good five minutes on each, to get them loose from their roots. I didn't know what to do with them. The last thing I wanted to do was smoke them. It was 1970, and in those days, laws regarding marijuana were strict, and I knew if I got caught, I was headed to the slammer. I stuffed them into three garbage bags and threw it into the car trunk. While driving away, even through the trunk, the skunky smell of the plants was overpowering. I was scared to death a cop might pull me over. I could already see headlines in the Merced Sun-Star:

Huge Pot Bust in Merced County

I made it to my friend Benny's house, and told him the story. He laughed, long and hard, then gladly took the plants off my hands. Benny was a heavy pot smoker, and being gifted homegrown Acapulco Gold plants was like hitting the mother lode. I just wanted out of there, away from all the illegal drug activity. "My hands, my clothes, the whole car smells like a giant skunk!" I complained. He was still laughing loudly as I drove away, peeling rubber.

The next day, I cleaned most of the smell out of the car with freshener and disinfectants. I kept thinking over and over about the trouble I almost got Daddy in. What if the police had raided the house and found the illegal plants? Knowing Daddy, he'd never give me up, and would take the rap for me. That would've broke my heart, because it was my fault, and he meant the world to me.

I thought again about the look on Daddy's face when he first told me about the plants. Daddy took real good care of them, watering them, watching over them like they were babies. That's when it hit me. These were his babies, his prized babies. The look on Daddy's face that day, was the look of a proud papa. No doubt about it, Daddy had a green thumb.

Sheriff White and his staff 1926, Merced, CA (Merced County Historical Society Archives)

San Francisco Farmer's Market (Alemany) circa 1950 (San Francisco History Center, SF Public Library)

Magic Kingdom

Since midweek we've been picking and packing produce for Saturday's haul to the San Francisco Farmer's Market. On the days leading to Friday, we'd take smaller loads to the house, and stack them in the garage. Fridays were the longest work days, because after we loaded the truck in the field, we had to also load the boxes at the house. Loading the truck for the trip usually didn't finish until around 9pm.

On Fridays the work was slightly different for me, because after our long lunch break, I'd be in charge of cutting the greens. These greens were the small end-tails that sprouted from the main plants of the okra and the opo (white squash). The greens were cut, bunched together with a rubber band, then packed into large crates.

Buying produce at SF Farmer's Market, circa 1960 (photo courtesy Lourdes Dumpit Clesson)

These were specialty items that had to be cut late on Friday afternoons, to maintain freshness for Saturday sales. I'd fill about twelve crates of these greens that sold for fifty cents a bunch. No matter how many I cut, they always sold out.

Tomatoes, okra, bitter melons, and long chilies were packed in wooden lugs. Bell peppers, cucumbers and small chilies were packed in cardboard boxes with lids. Larger stuff like squash (not greens), watermelons, sweet potatoes, eggplants and the various green toppings, were packed in bigger wooden crates.

By late afternoon, my brother Junie pulled the flatbed onto the field to load the stacked boxes at the end of the rows. Junie was in charge of loading, especially on Fridays, because we had to pack everything for maximum loads. Whatever didn't fit on the truck on Fridays was left behind. The truck had high rails, so we could put a lot on, then tie it down on all sides.

Going to the Farmer's Market in San Francisco on Saturday was like a reward for our hard work during the week. Junie drove the Wednesday loads, and Daddy usually took the Saturdays. If any of us kids wanted to go, including my sisters, we had to take turns. I always wanted to go. These trips to San Francisco with Daddy were great adventures. Daddy told many stories, and somewhere along the drives he'd find time to gently point out life lessons.

Our loaded-down truck inched its way out of town in the morning darkness, and rolled onto the 99, headed north. We drove through Atwater, Livingston, Turlock, then veered off down Maze Boulevard in Modesto towards Tracy. By the time the sun peeked through, the Bay Bridge was in sight. If I fell asleep on the way, Daddy woke me up, because he knew how excited I would get to see the big bridge and ocean. Halfway across the bay, I could see the first signs of skyscrapers. It was a dazzling sight, like seeing a Magic Kingdom poking through the fog. We pulled into the stands in back with the rest of the trucks, and stepped out into a wet fog mist. Daddy checked the load one more time, and then we walked behind the stands to a restaurant and store called the Farmer's Market Arcade for toast, eggs, and hot chocolate. It amazed me how it could be blistering summer heat in Merced, but here we had to wear a sweater or coat.

When we got back to the truck to unload, Mrs. Padua came out from the front of the stand to greet us. Mrs. Padua was the Filipina saleslady Daddy hired who lived in San Francisco. She took care of the stand during the week. While she and Daddy made small talk, I started unloading boxes and stacking them near the entrance. We never unloaded everything, only what was needed as it was sold during the day.

Kids eating watermelon at SF Farmer's Market (Alemany), circa 1950 (San Francisco History Center, SF Public Library)

Junie and Daddy made sure to load the truck according to items needed first at the front, or that were easy to get to from the top.

Little by little, the rest of the produce trucks came in, parked, and started unloading their own boxes. I recognized a few of the Filipino farmers by their trucks, so I knew they'd arrived. Produce at the Farmer's Market came from all over the valley. The crops coming from Merced was a small group of Filipino farmers the Hullanas, Dumpits, Acostas, Hidalgos, Balanons and us. It was like a Filipino fraternity from Merced. We grew mostly the same crops, but they had their own stands and display, scattered across the big lot. We didn't mingle too much because we were all too busy selling and restocking. The crowds came trickling in, and soon became a mass of people and lively bartering.

At the end of the day, most of the fog that burned off earlier started making its way back, which also meant it was time to start loading the truck for home. If it was a good Saturday, every box reloaded in the truck was empty.

SF Golden Gate Bridge in fog (photo courtesy Robert Lee Haycock)

Once we got everything loaded, Daddy and Mrs. Padua counted the money. Then we said our goodbyes and headed back to Merced. Sometimes Daddy stopped in Oakland to a part of town that had ducks hanging in the windows. Daddy, Junie and I, loved chopped-up duck with white rice. Most of the time, we'd just head straight out, and not stop until we got to Modesto, where we'd eat at this cool joint along the 99 that served giant burgers. After that, it was the home stretch to Merced.

As I got older, I realized this place wasn't the Magic Kingdom of my youthful days. San Francisco was just what it was, the big city. Daddy's been gone for many years, and I haven't been to that Farmer's Market in decades. Yet if I stop to think about it, I can see it clearly. The fog swirling around the Golden Gate and Bay Bridges, giant buildings, a million people talking at once, waving, wanting tomatoes, and bell peppers fresh off the Central Valley vine, and we're holding up fingers, yelling prices.

Most of all though, I remember those long drives rattling home down the freeway in the flatbed truck with Daddy. I can see his smiling round face, his twinkling eyes, and we're singing silly, made-up songs, and laughing. Warm, loving memories. A different kind of magic.

Bartering with customers at SF Farmer's Market (Alemany), circa 1960 (photo courtesy Lourdes Dumpit Clesson)

View from SF Bay Bridge to city of San Francisco and Golden Gate Bridge (photo courtesy Robert Lee Haycock)

Selling to two little girls at SF Farmer's Market (Alemany), circa 1950 (San Francisco Historical Center, SF Public Library)

SF Farmer's Market (Alemany)

during summer months
the crops from our humble patch
burst through the dirt and sand
tomatoes, potatoes, peppers,
as bountiful produce
to pick, pack and ship
from Merced,
to San Francisco Farmer's Market

Daddy got up early Saturdays
to haul our week's toil to The City
some days,
he let me ride along

he'd wake me at 4am
bundle me into the truck
and we'd rattle the old International
down the 99 to Modesto,
veer off to Maze boulevard,
through Tracy, all the way
to the Bay Bridge

i was about ten,
and Daddy was my world
every funny story, every secret,
he told me on these long rides

the Farmer's Market in San Francisco,
the ocean, skyscrapers, millions of people,
and that mysterious rolling fog,
was like going to Disneyland

we set-up colorful displays
for fruits and vegetables stands
to street-vend, side by side
with other Filipino farmers, friends,
the Castros, Dumpits, Hullanas,
Balanons, and Hidalgos
from Merced

SF Farmer's Market: SF Farmer's Market (Alemany) open area, circa 1960 (photo courtesy Lourdes Dumpit Clesson)

at the end of day,
the fog and cold seeping in,
we loaded the truck,
and inched our way back through traffic
by the time we hit the toll booth
at the Bay Bridge, i'd be asleep

Daddy'd shake me awake
in Modesto, our regular stop
to refuel and eat
at this cool place next to the 99,
that sold burgers for 10-cents,

i'd order two,
with a huge choc'let shake,
then go back to sleep,
as we rattled home
with a truckload
of empty boxes

Late Summer

Rode my ten-speed down G street, turned right at Child's Avenue, then left at Los Banos Highway. The field was on Gerard Avenue this year, about a half mile out of town. It was Friday, late summer in Merced. Daddy told me this morning to make sure I went to the field after school, because we needed me to help with the late pack.

When I got to Gerard, I stopped at the canal, took off my sweaty t-shirt, dipped it into the water, then put it back on to cool off. I looked up at the long rows of drying bell pepper plants in front of me, then off towards the back end, near the chilies and okra. I could see Daddy crouched low, wearing his familiar floppy hat, filling a box. My brother Junie was nowhere in sight, so Daddy was alone.

I walked my bike over to him. "Hi Daddy, what'd you want me to do first?" He looked up at me, the sun and countless years had taken a toll on his tired, burnt face.

"Ahh Charlie Boy, good that you came. Your brother went to the store to get a soda, and that was two hours ago," he said frustrated.

"He probably met a girl there," I said, "gave her ride." He just looked at me, and shook his head.

We've been filling the loads for the San Francisco Farmer's Market all summer, but the season was winding down. The crops were thinning, the loads smaller, and school had started again. Most of the work this time of year fell on Daddy. The only one who wasn't going to school was Junie, my oldest brother, and according to Daddy, was taking a long break.

I walked up to Daddy, smiled, then hugged him tight. He looked angry at first, then smiled at me. "How was school today? Don't forget your promise to do good in school. I don't want you anywhere near these fields when you grow up." It was the same lecture he gave me often. I'd do good alright, but only to please him. What I really wanted more than anything in the world was to grow up strong and hardworking like him, a farmer.

"I need you to finish picking the sweet potatoes on the far corner, then see if you can find some crates for the squash, it's already cut, just needs to be boxed. When you get done there, start bringing all the rest of the boxes to the end of the rows so you and your brother can load up," he said. He gave me a hug, then crouched into the row and went back to work.

Fridays were the days we needed to gather everything up for the market. Took us a little longer to get full loads this time of year, the crops were lighter, so we had to drag our boxes further through the rows to fill them. In a few weeks Daddy would declare the season officially

done. Junie would get out the old Farmall tractor and start plowing the plants under.

We never farmed the same patch of land the next year. Daddy said the soil needed to rest after we used it, so we were always relocating. It was common knowledge among the Filipino farmers in our town, not to farm the same produce every year on the same ground. It was nomad farming. Daddy scouted for patches of land all over Merced County the year before, then negotiated a contract with the landowners for the following year.

It started getting dark sooner now, so about 6:00 the sun was already cooling. I heard a loud honk from my brother Junie in the flatbed, as he turned into the field, raced towards me, then stopped bringing a huge cloud of dust. "Charlie Boy! Am I glad you're here, I thought I was going to have to load by myself," he said smiling. "Where've you been? I asked. "You left Daddy alone to get the Friday load ready?" I scolded. He's my big brother, but sometimes he acts years younger. "Got hung up man," he answered. "Yeah, what's her name?" He looked at me sideways, and laughed.

We started hustling the boxes on the flatbed. For being this late in season, we still had close to fifty boxes to load. About thirty minutes later, my younger brother Jimmy showed up. He went straight to Daddy's side of the field to help him finish packing. Eventually we drove the truck over to them to load the rest of the boxes.

"Let's go Daddy," I told him, "getting dark." He straightened up with a painful grunt, then walked over to us. He poured some water from the jug on his bandana and cooled his face. "Where'd you go?" Daddy said, looking at my

brother, "you know we have to get this load for tomorrow?" "Aw Daddy, I got hung up," Junie whined. I looked over at Junie and laughed. Daddy mumbled a few choice words in Filipino, then walked to the other truck with Jimmy.

With the flatbed fully loaded, I threw my bike in back, and climbed on top. We made our way to the front of the gate, then I yelled, "Junie stop!" He hit the brakes hard, and all the boxes shuffled and squealed forward. I jumped off the truck, stripped off my shirt and shoes, and dove into the canal for one last dip. Junie was blasting The Wolfman Jack Show on the truck radio, while he waited for me.

I ran back soaking wet. "Man, I needed that!" Junie popped the clutch, and angled the truck onto the road as I closed the gate. There were more boxes to load at the house on Cone Avenue, so we weren't done yet.

"OOOUUU! OOOUUU!" Wolfman was howling like crazy, embarrassing some chick on the radio, as we drove down Gerard in the darkness.

Bus Stop

Now that I've got a little time to read lately, I've run across other writers, who sort of share the same page as me. Not saying we write the same, but their upbringing, the area they're from, are similar. Chicano writers from California, the hot Central Valley fields that spin out both sides of Highway 99. Feels like, I'm reading me.

In this one bio, a well-known writer from Fresno speaks eloquently of another from that area, and shares stirring lines from his book. He goes on to mention other Chicano writers of that area, noteworthy and famous, rattling off a who's who list. It feels almost like I'm deliberately excluded from this private, very distinguished club. "Hey, what about me? I was born in the valley, I been writing since forever, my skin is brown, don't I rate?" Apparently a few

decades back, this rickety old bus rolled up, and I wasn't on it.

That's the problem when you dig a deep hole in your youth, and are too afraid to come out. Is it as simple as that, lack of courage? These writers paid their dues, boldly marched into the teeth of adversity, while I watched safely from behind a shaking bush. They deserve recognition, and rewards. And me, well it's a lonely, isolated bus stop.

Wish I was young again, and could look up the esteemed writers of my generation, follow their lead to exhilarating heights and inspiration. I'd talk about watching from the car window as a child, while my father worked the asparagus fields in Ballico. I'd talk about picking tomatoes and bell peppers on Lingard Way just off the 99. I'd talk about working the big chicken ranches for Foster Farms, or tying grape vines in winter with my father, then picking the same grapes for Gallo in summer.

Rolo's bus (photo Rudy Cuellar RCAF)

I'd talk about fishing the canals and rivers like Bear Creek, Black Rascal, Penny Hole and Catfish Junction. I'd talk about being busted, spending three months in Merced County Road Camp (MCRC). I'd talk about saving Gilbert from drowning at Shaffer Bridge near Winton. I'd mention that I was raised on welfare, and grew up in the projects. I'd talk about being hit by a train at eighteen on G street in Merced and living to write about it. I'd lay it all out there, page after page, a lost and squandered lifetime of missed opportunities, failed dreams, and prove to all of them, I'm not invisible, I've got stuff to write!

Then, just like that, some poisonous old snake slithers in my shirt, up my back and neck, and whispers, "Hey man, you just ain't good enough." Yeah, well that's tough to swallow.

The valley sun scorches my face to a blistering peel as I sit on a wooden box on the side of the road. Buses coming, going...never stop.

Plane cropdusting field, Merced County (Merced County Historical Society Archives)

The Recorder (2008)

How many times have I walked back and forth in this room? Denial is a strange beast. Need to go backward, in order to go forward. Take out those scribbled notes of two years ago, relive the sadness of my brother's death. Lots of notes. Why do I do this? Why bother?

Started gathering all the notes this morning. Those days, especially Junie's last week when he lay on that bed breathing by machine only. It was surreal. That wasn't him, it was someone else.

I must have sat down everywhere to jot notes. That was my only safe place. It was the year before that we'd lost Mama. The wounds from her loss cut deep. And the time years before, when Daddy's death, nearly killed me. I know, because I wrote it down.

I didn't want to write about this, didn't want to write about losing anyone in my family. That kind of reality isn't worth recording. Or is it? In my notes I even jot the exact time of day, as well as the date. As if that will make a difference ten years down the road. Is that what I'm supposed to do, be there to record immense pains, tragic loss?

I already know to get where I'm going with this, I'll have to spend a few hours going over October 2006. Alone in those safe places, parked in my car, lobbies, hallways, coffee shops.

Tio Frank, Grandpa "Papa," Tio Boogie, Tio Charlie

On the road dealing, reeling, agonizing, recording. Didn't make sense then, barely does now.

I suppose someone's got to do it. I suppose if I hadn't written it down, the moments leading to his last breath, the grieving, the burial, all of it, would be lost forever. I doubt anyone would care. I'm here for reason, scribbling notes, insignificant lines in the sand, as if it will all make sense someday.

So today I'll write my brother's ending finally, because I've decided it's time. I wonder though, if that's what I'm supposed to do, record each loved ones family history through death. Who will record me? Doesn't matter really, I'll be gone. My life drama will finally have and ending.

"He, who wrote for all, died today."

This Winter

I suppose, with the wind and rain outside, and more to come, we've cocooned with blankets, warm fires. I suppose like the change of season, freezing cold, instead of sun, inward, instead of outward. The season of that endless war, killer hurricanes, loved ones lost. Turn the page, start over

I've often wondered if I'm a winter writer, rather than summer. Throw on thick sweaters, coats, gloves and trek high up the mountain to my tower, to "bear" for winter. One small, frosty window to look out. "Countless tales to be told," I write in my journal, shivering, "layers of rain, snow, and wind, to overcome."

It is this imagination that binds the ones who write. With pen in hand, or fingers spread evenly on a keyboard. Wipe the frost, find the pulse. Tell them what ails, or inspires. Reveal the colors, be it agony, intense and miserably cold, or thoughts of romance, desires engulfed or enflamed by simple candlelight. Set the temperature and tone, open the page, begin.

I suppose, from my mountain view, the lights below, mere weeks before Christmas, that I've got something significant to share. A vast landscape, glistening jewels of lights, smoke billowing from thousands of chimneys. Don't know, can't tell yet. Maybe nothing.

I stroke my long beard, smoke my pipe, pull the flaps of my hat lower. We are, the words of every season, all of us, to our last breath, touching hearts and souls, scribbling blindly, breathlessly, designing, building, hunkering down.

But all is silent, save the wind, howling at my back.

Look, tell them of the pain of death so recently endured, what my eyes have seen, tortured, beaten, abused. Tell them of flying high above the fray, a view so magnificent, it begs to say, to express, to share. Create an unforgettable character, that mighty hero of mind and heart that gives, saves, knows all. One who carries us to that tearful page of victory. Lie down here, another blanket to keep warm.

I suppose, there is no greatness, not now, perhaps later, but we trudge through, press on. Every day, every season, different.

High above the howling storm, frost on my beard, eyes searching wanefully to heartfelt losses, human touch. Seasons that follow, lead, churn deeply. Imagination does not go cold. Or does it? Here, take this pen, write it. Eyes, alive and moving beyond the snow, conjuring winters across the ridge, snowflakes dreamily to the page.

We're not gone, only adjusting, acclimating, different sight and sounds, binding. Takes time to see, peel the layers, undress. There is nothing to say, not yet, the world at our feet.

"Countless tales," I write, "layers of rain, snow, and wind, to overcome."

Yosemite/Plainsburg Rd exit towards Planada

Piece Work   Slices of Life

Where Old Tractors Go To Die (Bright's in LeGrand)

Tractor graveyard on Plainsburg Road (photo by Jasmin Mariano)

driving down Plainsburg road
just off the 99
on an overcast, early eve
miles and miles
of orchards, fields

from a distance,
could make out shapes
long lines of something,
ghostly silhouettes,
in the middle of nowhere

i stopped, for a better view
and stared
at rows and rows
of old tractors, lined up
solemnly,
tires flat, treads broken, rusted

a once mighty army
chugging, clanking loudly,
silenced,
brought to a standstill

no more ground to cultivate,
a final resting place

just before the sun sank
into an ominous
dusky haze,

i thought about all the old farmers
gone now,
on these great machines
who bled, sacrificed, worked the land
under that brutal, central valley sun,
side by side,

with my father

(photo Diana Mariano)

THE HOUSE ON 12TH

growing up in Merced
various rentals, all rundown
the most memorable, 107 West 12th
the address engraved in my mind
the white house at the corner,
with the cracked front window, wooden porch,
the willow and chinaberry trees on the side
a half block from the 99, on 13th
across the street, opposite direction
the holy roller church, and a block further
to the cyclone fence surrounding
the Merced Fairgrounds on 11th
near Papa Alonzo's house, next door
to my godparents, Adela and Juan Vega
everyone and everything, near and around us
Huiars on the left, Campos behind us,
Porras on the right, Velasquez down the alley,
Valdez a half block from there, near La Perla store
down 12th, two blocks left, G Street Tavern,
a block from there, the Madayags,
going right, towards J street
Buyright Liquors, Beacons, to Food Center
where i walked barefoot a thousand times,
to buy Abba Zabbas, and Big Hunk bars
Javier Solis on the record player,
food constantly steaming on the stove,
chasing Lola through the house,
swinging, slamming the torn screen door,
dogs barking, Mama yelling

i stare now, towards the lights of the fairgrounds,
and the emptiness of all it used to be
the swirling dust from the car races,
the giant cactus that surrounded grandpa's house
like a fortress, smells from the kitchen,
sopas, beans de la olla, and fresh rolled torts,
early evenings, sitting on the porch in Mama's
lap, telling her all about my wild adventures,
holding tight

when i dream, i dream this house

Mama and cousin Becky, 1963

FOOTPRINTS

Mama

don't want to get into
why
it felt so bad
that we were poor

why
i wore ugly shoes
and pants
that fit too big
with holes

that brown duplex
on 12th and K
we lived in,

government housing
for those
woefully without

why
it bothered me
yesterday

when i drove by
saw every building
leveled
an empty lot

i stopped
took it all in
the air
hauntingly quiet

it's all gone now
like Mama
and my childhood
nothing's forever

family gatherings
Mama cooking up a storm
in that small kitchen

the black neighbors
the Martins,
the Harrises
magnificently poor,
like us

shared tables
best friends

a variety of music
Trio Los Panchos,
Nat King Cole,
James Brown,
blared
out our windows

the sweet smell
of capirotada
and barbecue
wafting, curling

a framed picture
of JFK
next to the Virgin Mary
a lit candle
in the middle

Thanksgiving, Christmas,
countless birthdays
that ugly house
filled to the brim
with warm memories
every loving inch

don't want to get into
why
this empty lot
bothers me
why my chest aches
for every last
precious piece

i see Mama
at the window
her foodstained apron
hair in bobbypins
her scarf
wrapped tight around her head
like Aunt Jemimah,

waving goodbye

(artwork Mareia de Socorro, Co-Madres Artistas de Sacra)

Sunday Visit

we sit
in Mama's kitchen
at the projects on seventh

the windows
steamed
from coffee, menudo
and cigarettes

sweat,
pours from my forehead
as i dig into
a hot bowl of menudo

Tio Boogie
Tia Ofelia and Mama,
on a roll, dishing on
the latest Merced dirt,
tramps, two-timers, killers

i fold my tortilla
dip it into the menudo,
add chili

the radio plays
old Mexican tunes
from the 50's and 60's

the three of them
reminiscing
back and forth,
the good old days

Tio Boogie rolls his eyes
floats dreamily to his heyday,
when he was Cassius Clay,
and Fred Astair,
rolled into one,

a fabulous career
that barely missed
the bigtime

Tia Ofelia
the youngest sister
wears a scarf
to hide the baldness
from chemo,
laughs at a picture of herself
at ten
sitting on a horse

Mama, Tia Dela, Tia Lupe

there's a picture of Daddy
and Mama
holding baby Junie
by the big bell
at Applegate Park,
his skin
sunburned dark
floppy hat, white t-shirt

Mama's long black hair
combed high in a bun,
like the Andrew Sisters

Mama said,
Grandma died that year,
and how Grandpa
used to beat her badly,
and often

Javier Solis croons,
"Y Volver, Volver, Volverrr!"

Tio Boogie grabs the broom
to dance, starts singing
Tia Ofelia sings with him,
sways dreamily

Mama wipes the sweat
off my forehead
with her apron,
serves me another bowl,
and warms up more tortillas

Tia Ofelia, cousin Lupita, cousin Natalia

CACTUS HOUSE

A couple of weeks ago I decided to gather most of the old black and white pictures of my family and spread them out on the back table. It was to see which ones I had copies of, and try to organize them better. I walk by the pictures ten or fifteen times a day now and it seems there's always something I didn't notice before. Of course the centerpiece of all my photos are Mama in countless poses at all ages. In most of my favorite pictures, she's holding a baby. I never realized that until now.

The interesting thing is in these old pictures of Mama, is at various ages of her life, she resembles my brother, sisters, aunts, cousins, even me. She's all our faces. Her face is the look of innocence and beauty, regardless of the poverty around her. Some of the houses are wooden shacks, straight out of the Depression era. I stare into her familiar eyes in one old photo, and can almost feel the baby reaching out to me. Yes, Mama and all her babies.

I met with my friend Laura, who is an artist and photographer, at Lyon's restaurant Saturday morning to go over a few images needed for this book. I was about to tell her about the photos of Mama holding babies, when I stopped and had one of those, "Shoulda had a V-8" moments. There was a second recurring theme in those pictures. "Nopales! I said loudly, "big cactus!" Laura looked at me confused, and smiled, "We can do that." "Not just nopales," I added, "but cactus clustered tightly together and climbing high. Big, giant cactus."

When I got back, I picked through the stack of old pictures again, and there it was, a cactus everywhere. It wasn't just any cactus, or any house, it was my grandfather Augustine's house. Everyone called him 'Papa.' Papa's house was on 11th street, behind the Merced Fairgrounds. This house and lot, was surrounded by giant cactus, so whenever anyone took pictures, cactus was practically in every background shot.

Here's a photo of grandma Socorro and Mama holding a baby, the cactus towering behind them. Here's another of tia Dela posing in a skirt and fur coat, and another of Mama in the back yard holding an oversized picture of the Virgin Mary. There's a tore-up couch and old tire on the ground, and to the left of her, imposing giant cactus.

Mama

The cactus at that house were as tall as the house and such a common sight back then, that most of us just didn't see it anymore. It was like the lawn, or the bushes growing on the side of the house. Papa planted the cactus long before I was born, so by the time I noticed it as a small boy, they were gigantic. He grew them close together, which I'm sure was a form of home security, because only an idiot would crawl through that prickly fortress, they'd be cut to ribbons.

The house on 11th was leveled over twenty years ago, and is now apartments. The cactus are gone too, but I'm sure they're still there, like armed ghosts, still patrolling the property. Mama, and most of the relatives in these old photos, are gone too now. They only exist in my aches and longings. Like today, when I pull the pictures out, spread them lovingly around me. Mama, the babies and the cactus, a nice, warm blanket.

Tia Dela, Tia Concha Sarabia, Grandma Socorro, cousin Natalia

Nopales (photo by Laura Llano)

SHOES

shoes
say who you are
where you're from
Converse, Nike,
best money can buy

when i was a kid,
a mocoso,
from the K street projects
in Merced,

my shoes
were like my skin
dirty, callused, peeling

i wore shoes
from the segunda,
secondhands, for a buck

wore them
till they barked
flopping front ends
patched with tape
cardboard insoles

nothing to do
with culture,
everything to do
with poor

don't recall
being dirty, smelling bad,
or crying,
but must have

i remember hungry
a lot

and no matter
how many times
i changed the cardboard
in my shoes
embarrassed
by my hardened, unwashed socks,
or wondered why
everyone in school
stared,

i'd just lower my head
pretend not to notice,
then go home
to our house
in the projects,
where it was safe
where everyone
wore shoes,

like me

Tortillas and Bread

"I didn't know you were so…
Mexican,"
a friend told me,
offhandedly

"oh really, why's that?"
i said

"well, this music, those people,
the way your toe's tapping
to the beat,"
she answered
"i just thought,
you weren't part of that"

"part of what?"
i said, playing along

"you know, like those lowlifers…"
"lowriders," i corrected

"whatever…they're out there,
dancing all crazy, probably drunk,"
she pointed out

"my grandparents
on my mother's side,
came from Mexico,
desperately poor, but hardworking,
proud Americans,

and toe-tapping
to this beautiful,
heartfelt music,
takes me home"

"oh. i just never saw you as,
you know…real Mexican,"
she said

i stared into her sweet,
ignorant face, and smiled,

"really? why is that…?"

(photo by Trent Harger)

TIO MIKE

it was around Christmas
we still lived
in the brown projects
on K street, Merced

i remember the phone
ringing loudly, woke me
it was raining
cats and dogs

Mama screamed
into the phone

poked my head out
just in time
to see her race out
into the rain

she picked up tias Adela, Ofelia, Molly,
and pregnant cousin Linda,
drove that rainslicked 99,
to LA

later, during that awful night
got word their car crashed,
but miraculously,
survived

they were rushed
to the very same hospital
as Tio Mike
were able see him,
hold his hand

Mama came home
bandaged, shaken,
broken nose,
couldn't stop crying

December 28, 1969
the night Linda's baby
was born
the night,
Tio Mike died

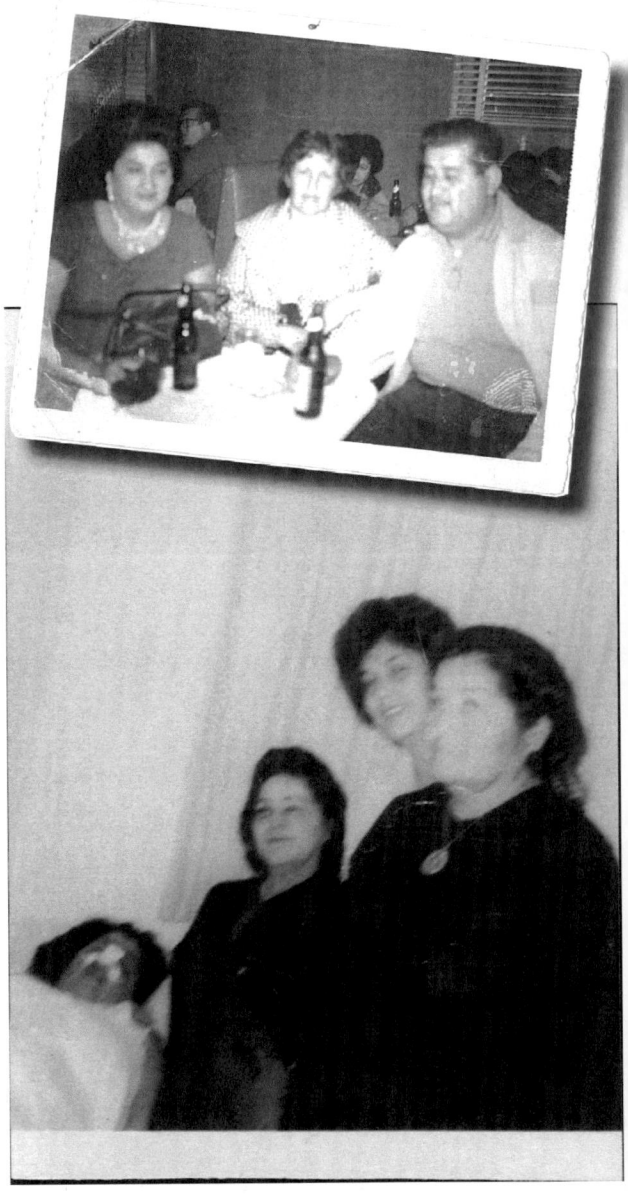

Top- Mama, Tia Molly, Tio Mike
Bottom- Mama (laying down in hospital bed),
Tia DelaTia Ofelia, Tia Lupe

The Artist (For Gilbert "Magu" Lujan)

waiting
for the phone to ring,
steam,
rises from my coffee cup

the phone call
from my dear friend
who's dying,
but refuses to go
without a fight

it's become clear to me
now,
he's leaving

tried to believe
he'd make this
miracle comeback
believe,
like he believed,
but i knew

his dazzling, distinctive
artwork,
that fills this room
framed on my walls,
our wild, spirited talks
constant sharing,
soon silenced

"orale hermano!"
his voice scratchy, barely there,
"can only talk a few minutes...tired"

we argued,
got all worked up
then laughed,
about these two
pitiful old dudes,
crying like babies

The Snake Lady (2008)

Note from my cousin, Josie Cervantes:

"Hello Primo, I've been thinking about you a lot since I last saw you at tia Molly's 86th birthday bash at the American Legion. I remembered something you wrote last year and it made me think of tia Molly and how great it would be for you to write about her before she passes. I'm so amazed how she's out-lived all of our mothers, and was there for them all up until their end. I see her smiling face and all these fond memories float through my head, so many. I always remember seeing her with a can of Coors, trying to dance and kiss everyone. She's so funny. Do you remember all the times she'd come from Fresno to help your mother cook for weddings or gatherings? I'm so glad I was able to tell her how much I love her. How sad the day will be when we lose the last of the Mohicans in our family."

Last weekend the family met at the American Legion Hall in Merced for Tia Molly's 86th birthday. Tia Molly was married to my mom's brother Mike Alonzo, and represents the last of the tias from that generation. Wish Mama was there. She would've liked this party.

I'm at an age now where the older generation that I've shared and enjoyed is slowly ending. My generation will soon replace them and become the older generation. Tia Molly is a precious link to that time, a time when we're all still kids growing up; first loves, first communions, marriages, babies, lots of babies. There's still a few of the originals left: Tio Boogie in Merced, Tio Charlie in Los Angeles, Tio Frank in Planada, and Tia Molly in Fresno. I don't think of us as a family tree, we're more like a giant cactus, with lots of espinas (stickers) on it.

When I walked through the front door of the American Legion, my heart warmed seeing all the family faces. For once, the family isn't jarred by a tragic loss, another funeral. I made my way to Tia Molly for a birthday hug, and she got up and planted a wet kiss on my cheek. "Hi Tia, happy birthday," I tell her. "Ay Mijo," she says, "every time I sit down, there's another beer for me." She holds my hand and laughs.

After a dance with cousin Ponchie, she sits down for a rest and talks with me. "Did you know I worked in the circus?" she said. With all the noise, I thought I heard wrong.

"What? Can't hear Tia," I yelled back, "Sounded like you said you were in the circus."

"Yeah Mijo," she answered, "I was the Snake Lady."

"Yeah, right Tia, good one," I laughed. Then she got up to go dance again.

I went to talk with my sister Lola to ask her about the circus thing. I was pretty sure Tia had one too many Coors already. "She's got a picture," Lola said.

"No way!" I said. I made a mental note to check later.

The next day at Lola's house, I got a hold of that photo and of Tia Molly, and I sat with her on the sofa to get the lowdown straight from the Snake Lady's mouth. "So Tia, you say you were in this circus. What circus?" I asked.

"L&G Barnes Circus," she answered, "We toured all over California, even Colorado. I was The Snake Lady for three years, and used two different snakes, a boa and a python." Suddenly, this crazy story started sounding legit. I shook my head in amazement.

I stared at the old black and white photo dated June 21, 1933. It's a group shot of six adults and one little girl, about two years old, in front. Standing second from the right, is 23-year old Tia Molly with a long striped dress and white collar. You can tell it's her, because she's the spitting image of her daughter, my cousin Chilly.

"There were other attractions, the trapeze act,

Standing first left, Emilia Huizar. Standing middle, Tia Molly. Sitting front, Joe Lopez (Fire-Breathing Man). Little girl in front, cousin Kathy (photo Tia Molly Alonzo)

motorcycle act, fire-breathing man, the fat lady, clowns, elephants, tigers, and 2 bears," she says. She goes on to tell me about some of the others in that photo. The little girl is my cousin Kathy. The man kneeling directly behind Kathy is Joe Lopez, The Fire-Breathing Man. Joe Lopez and Lucilla Romero, The Fat Lady, baptized Kathy. The woman to the far left, I recognized as a longtime friend of Tia Molly and Mama, Emilia Huizar. Her son Raymond was in my class at Galen Clark Elementary, and their family lived across the street from us on 12th street.

"I used to handle the snakes for the crowd to see, while a barker in a red hat told stories. One time there was this black lady walking back and forth, putting her hands up to touch the snake. I told her not to put her hands there, or she'd get bit, but she kept doing it. I saw the snake coil to bite, so I stuck my hand out in front to protect her, and it bit me. I was taken to San Francisco Hospital to treat the bite."

Tia Molly was also part of the motorcycle act. "The motorcycle would rise out of a door open at the bottom, go all the way up, then down into a tunnel of rings, then ride on a rope. Eventually the motorcycle rider would ask for a volunteer from the audience. If no once came forward, I'd volunteer and would get on back. One time I fell, and the motorcycle landed on me. I had to stay at Merced General Hospital for a week."

I think back to Tia Molly's 86th birthday party at the American Legion, and the DJ's blasting the song "Mustang Sally." When the song gets to the main chorus, the whole bar is clapping and cheering, singing loudly, "Mustang Molly!" Tia does a twirl, a side step, and a back step, all in slow-mo.

After the song ended, she raised her arms triumphantly to wild applause, and bows. As usual, Tia Molly takes the cake.

Piece Work — Slices of Life

*Vernon's Drive-In at 1035 W. 16th Street, circa 1950
(Merced County Historical Society Archives)*

OVERPLAYED

i tend to
disappear
in spots
far
from the limelight

which is funny
because
i'm not in any light

so i retract
retreat
fadeaway,
for months

not a peep
not a word

sometimes,
i feel
like an old 45
on the record player
spinning,
playing constantly

the needle
pressed into the grooves
plays to the end
the arm lifts,
replays

over and over,
until the grooves
turn white,
the music
scratchy,

skipping

JFK whistle-stop Merced,
September 9, 1960
(Merced County Historical Society Archives)

Filling station, Merced County, circa 1940

Farming

was told recently,
"you have an amazingly
fertile mind"

"really," i said,
"you mean like
growing squash
or corn?"

a farmer
prepares the ground
cultivating
long, even furrows
nurturing seeds
to sprouts

then at sunrise
long under
a blistering sun
inserts small plants
six inches apart
into the moist soil

"yes, my mind seems fertile,
bursting
through the dirt
sweat and sun,
spread over
a vast, rich earth,
but in reality
it's the fertilizer
bountiful and plenty,
that i'm full of"

Turkey farm, Merced County 1960 (Merced County Historical Society Archives)

Rearview

most of my
youthful years
i've had these books
novels,
intriguing, greatest stories
never told, never read,
living in my head

the first decades
entered, reentered
as mysterious,
adventurous dreams

now,
as the years
gathered into a heap
the books
that swirled, danced wildly,
are flailing,
gasping for breath

waited too long

these books
magically delicious
throughout
sadly,
will never see
the light of day,

so when i die
i'll just stack them
into neat little piles,
and take them with me

Highway 99 sign, view from Gerard Avenue, Merced (photo by Jasmin Maximus)

THE 99

my family
miserably poor
inching south, scratching north
up and down the 99,
every dogtown
in between
Merced, Madera, Fresno,
Livingston, Modesto, Stockton

towns
just off the freeway
small, dusty, hot

tomato fields, grape fields,
chicken plants,
scrubbing floors, toilets

we lived, survived,
near the on-ramps
every town

"for fast getaways," i'd say,
"case the cops were chasin"

Daddy,
dusk to dawn
tired, broken,
wilted,
under that blistering sun

the 99,
ever-present, streaming
left to right
a thick, pulsing,
smoky vein,

right down the middle

(Caltrafficsigns)

Benjamin Samuel

I used to consider myself the strong, silent type. I realized after growing up and leaving Merced to go to college, that two of my three brothers, Benjie and Jimmy, shared a similar personality trait, only in varying degrees. I was quiet, Jimmy was quieter, and Benjie, well Benjie was a whole different ballgame.

Benjie

Benjamin Samuel Mariano was two years older than me, and the one in the family that kept to himself the most. He was always mysterious... and secretive. Some of these secrets got him in trouble and locked up in Juvie a lot. Eventually he graduated to the California Youth Authority (CYA). I don't remember the order of his arrests and where he ended up first, but it seemed he was locked up in every CYA in California at some time or another. Nellis, Mt Bullion, Tracy, to name a few. When he got out, he'd disappear into the underworld, get in trouble, and go right back. Daddy, Mama, and the rest of us saw him more on our CYA visits, than we did when he was out.

Sometime during his first troubles with the law, Benjie decided to do away with his first name. I guessed it was because it didn't sound tough enough, especially around other criminals. He took his middle name Samuel, shortened it, and then told everyone in a direct, almost threatening manner, to call him "Sam." Without saying it out loud, you knew there was an 'or else,' attached to the request. Most people didn't dare cross that line. I'm not sure why, but I refused to call him "Sam." I continued to call him "Benjie," a dangerous move, even for a brother. I honestly believe he thought about beating me up a few times, then stopped, and let it slide. It was a silent agreement to let me live.

With each incarceration, he came back bigger, stronger, became an imposing presence. He'd come to the house to eat, but it was on his own time, and reason. By then, it was no secret he drank too much, and did lots of drugs. From the very beginning, every vice imaginable, he not only did it, he took it to the extreme.

Even the way he dressed, was ground-breaking for our town back in the early 60's. He wore the big baggy Frisco pants, with a white t-shirt and suspenders, and had a long chain hanging from his oversized wallet. His black hair was slicked back with pomade into a pompadour, and when he walked, he walked the walk.

Most of the cops in town knew him by first name, from all the arrests. As long as he wasn't causing any trouble, they left him alone. He'd paid his dues. He wasn't loud and showy, but was well known, and feared. He didn't run in gangs, he was a loner, an army of one. I've never known him to hurt or kill anyone, never witnessed it, but it wouldn't surprise me.

After a few years of settled life, he gained weight, let his hair grow out into a long pony-tail that went all the way to his butt. At the time, no one wore their hair long, so he stood out. He started wearing a small black derby too, and sported little square, wire-rimmed glasses, we called pimp-shades. A couple of my cousins nicknamed him Secret Sam. I remember walking into a few parties when I was a teenager back then, scared at first at the hard looks I got walking in, then later surprised when they came to me apologizing, after finding out I was Sam Mariano's brother. It was immediate street cred, without having any. Nobody, and I mean nobody, messed with Sam's brother.

His reputation toned down some in later years, long after his heyday. I'd come home and find him drunk on a chair at gatherings. He'd be the least noticeable person in any room. Never say a word, just kept quietly to himself, drinking steadily. One thing was certain, known by all family and friends, if he's in the room quiet like that, you don't dare disturb him. He was a ticking bomb.

After college, I decided to stay in Sacramento, so I saw Benjie even less. I'd drive home only on holidays, and he wouldn't be around. The first thing I asked, after spending time with family, was "Where's Benjie?" He didn't drop by the family much, and sometimes no one would see him for weeks or months. Being away so often, I missed him, wanted to bring him to the house, join in the family for the holidays, so I'd always go looking for him.

CYA Mt. Bullion visit. back row: Benjie, Connie (friend), Tia Nottie, Dolores, Daddy, Tio Joe front row: Diana, cousin Becky, cousin Josie, Johnny (friend)

By the time Benjie was in his forties, the hard life had taken a toll on his body. He had health problems, heart and high blood pressure. He was getting by on disability insurance and county assistance. When I came home for visits, I'd find him at a different place, living like a hermit, barely getting by.

On one of these visits about 1990, Christmas time, I asked Mama where he was staying this time, and she didn't know. I called my sister Lola, and she told me he was living in the old El Capitan Hotel, just off M street. I brought a box of clothes and food items, so around 9pm, I took off to El Capitan Hotel to give it to him. My main reason was to get him to come to the house for Christmas.

El Capitan used to be a fancy hotel in the heart of the city, but had seen better days by the time Benjie moved in. It was rooms to rent for low-income people. Benjie fit the bill. I knocked on the door of the second floor where he lived. He opened it, glared out at me, then smiled. "What's the haps Charlie Boy?" "Benjie, let's go to Mama's to grub down, there's tons of food." He barely showed half interest, so I prodded more. "C'mon man, just for a little while, I'll bring you back." I gave him the box, and he just shook his head, and gave up. "Go wait in the car. I'll be down in a minute."

I went downstairs to sit in the car and wait.

While waiting, I see two very large, scary-looking figures walking down the sidewalk about a block away, coming towards me. Both are wearing long, black leather coats. I quickly check the locks to make sure I'm secure. As they got closer, I recognized one of the guys from when we lived out on McGregor Avenue. I hadn't seen him in years. Last I heard he was in Folsom Prison for armed robbery. Despite being one of the town hard guys, and physically imposing, Lawrence always treated me good when his family lived next door to us. No doubt, because he dated my sister Dolores for a while. The other guy I recognized too, we called him 'Wolfman.' He was bad news, and also an ex-con. He used to run with my brother Benjie back when they were teenagers. He was big and sinister looking, with

2nd visit, Mt. Bullion. left to right: Jimmy Boy, Johnny (friend), Mama, me (in back), Benjie, Daddy, Diana (in front)

a face that was a mass of bumps and craters, with two beady eyes coming out of it. If it wasn't for Lawrence being with him, I'd be scared to death. I was glad to see Lawrence. Wolfman was ok, long as you kept your distance, watched your back. They came closer, then glared suspiciously into the car, sizing me up. I rolled down the electric window on their side.

"Lawrence! What's happening?" They stopped cold, look menacingly through the window, about to pounce. "It's me, Charlie," I tell him.

"Who you say ese?" says Wolfman, inching closer, reaching into his coat for something.

Lawrence's face lights up in a big smile, "Oh hey, it's Charlie! What's up homes, long time no see. How's Lola these days?"

"Yeah, I live in Sac, been gone a long time. Lola's with Chava now, still has the two boys," I tell him, "man Lawrence, you look huge."

"Lifting inside," he says.

Lawrence pokes his huge head through the window to shake my hand. Wolfman thinks about it awhile, then looks at me hard, then shakes my hand too. "Orale ese! Where you been?" He starts checking out my car, first outside, then the back seat. "Got any frajos?"

"Nahh man, I don't smoke."

Lawrence's face turns serious. "Hey bro, you looking good. Nice ride. What you doing out here?"

"Waiting for my brother Benjie," I tell him.

"Think you could lend us some cash? We're down thirty smacks and the dude's gonna split any time," says Lawrence.

Wolfman starts working the game, walking back and forth, checking both sides of the block for live bodies. He comes back and crowds in front with Lawrence, no longer asking, but intimidating. "Look ese, we need some cash bad, and we also need a lift. Throw us a ride to Oleander, soze we can get this deal done."

"Don't have any cash," I lied, "and gotta

get going anyways. Doing the family thing for Christmas, and already late."

Wolfman and Lawrence, getting agitated, pop the window locks and get inside anyway. Wolfman jumps in the back seat, Lawrence in front. "Let's go man! Damn Charlie, what's with you? Too good for your old time brothers?" Usually, I can talk my way out of this street nonsense, but these two looked too far gone for reasoning. It'd been too long between former friendships. Nothing was clicking. It was stupid of me to stop them to say hello, big trouble. My heart was racing, trying desperately to figure a way out.

"C'mon Lawrence, I told you I can't. You know my mom. She'll be pissed if I don't get there soon."

Lawrence glances down the long front entrance to the El Capitan Hotel. "Who'd you say you were waiting for Charlie?"

"My brother," I answered.

"Who's your damn brother?" snarled Wolfman.

"Benjie," I said.

"Benjie? Benjie who?"

"Mariano," I told him.

"Benjie Mariano?" Lawrence suddenly gets a flash. You mean Sam, Sam Mariano. That's who you're waiting for?"

Wolfman and Lawrence get wide-eyed, looking out the window towards the front entrance again, then back at me, like it was something they'd totally forgotten. "Sam's your brother?" said Wolfman, all excited, "and that's who you're waiting for right now?" They're yelling now, scrambling out of the car.

"Yeah, I told you that. What's wrong?" I say.

"We gotta go! Lawrence says loudly.

"Let's get the hell out of here!" Wolfman shouts, "tell Sam we were just messing around ok? We're cool, right homes?"

"Yeah, yeah, no problem," I tell them.

If I wasn't so damn scared, I would've fallen down laughing. I couldn't believe it. They hustled out the car quick, raced down the street, and disappeared in seconds. I was still shaking with fear and amazement when Benjie casually strolls out the door of the El Capitan, holding the empty box. He drops it in the back seat and climbs in front. "Let's go."

"Benjie, did you see those two guys running down the street. Did you see them?"

"No, what guys?"

"It was Wolfman and Lawrence trying to run a scam on me for money and a ride. When I told them I was waiting out here for you, they absolutely freaked, and ran like hell. It was crazy as hell."

Benjie, about 43 now, not as big as either of them, and way past the notorious image of my childhood, listened to what I said, then mumbled softly, but matter-of-factly, "They knew I'd kill 'em."

I started to laugh, then looked over at Benjie. He wasn't smiling.

That was all he said, the rest of the way to Mama's house. Once inside, a roomful of relatives erupted, standing in line to hug me. Mama practically cracks my ribs with a squeeze, then looks at my brother, shakes her head and rolls her eyes.

"Where's them enchiladas?" Benjie says, then slides by us into the kitchen.

Alzheimer's (2005)

driving home again
how many times?
hundreds?

this time,
for Mama

yesterday,
constant crying
i'm alright, we're alright,
stop crying

driving home again
the 99, south
'bout two hours

we were always poor
nothing to fight over
at the end

last month,
when she still could,
i asked tearfully,
"hey Mama, do you still love me?" she

looked at me, with that
thousand-mile stare,
opens her arms, kisses me,
"i'll always love you mijo"

"Mama?"

her eyes blinked, glistened,
then left

going home again,
deep breaths,

birds singing...all sad songs,

stop crying

Mama

First Rain (2007)

Seems like I'm always sitting down somewhere writing something about first rain. Summer is behind us, the cold and wind the last couple of days, then rain, hard rain. Time keeps coming, going.

Opened up a few envelopes stacked loosely in my bookcase. Things shoved in, because during the last move didn't know where else to put it. It's there, stacked with all the other thick manila folders. Stories, pictures, loose pieces from Merced.

What the hell, its raining. I opened one, a handful of pictures, articles cut and saved, grandpa's birth certificate, mine, moms. Baptism certificates, school report cards, copies of welfare forms, cards, receipts. Who, how, or why doesn't matter anymore.

Daddy and Mama at 'The Bell,' Applegate Park, Merced

Pulled out another stack of pages, pictures. Mama cooking at the lake. Mama cooking in the kitchen, at the park, at the Women's club. Mama at the family reunion. Mama when she was fourteen, Mama playing guitar outside grandpa's house, with pre-teens, Lupita, Ofelia and Natalia sitting around her. Mama sitting in the backyard swing with tia Molly crocheting. Mama at Melina's wedding. Mama at Christmas time, Mama about to cut into a shiny golden turkey, Mama in some crazy clown make-up on Halloween.

I opened another large manila envelope. Brother Junie as a baby, sitting on Grandma Soccoro's grave 1949. Junie holding baby Diana high on the front porch at the white house at 107th West 12th street. Brother Benjie with 11-year old Diana at 1231 K street, the projects, 1962. Me, holding baby Melina in front of the Christmas tree, Mama's house 1981.

The rain outside pounds the roof. Another envelope, more pictures spill out, scatter on the floor. Piles of pictures. Pictures of all of us, Inez, Jimmy, Junie, Dolores, Diana, Me, with Mama in front of the house on 7th street after brother Benjie's funeral. A group shot of a birthday at Yosemite Lake with Daddy. Daddy with Mama at the big bell at Applegate Park. A group shot of Mama, Tia Ofelia, Tia Dela, Tio Boogie, Tio Frankie, Tio Charlie in front of the projects on 7th street. A couple of years later, another group of all of them, after Tia Ofelia's funeral.

Another envelope, taken during Mama's hospice, April 2005. The pain in her face, in our faces, a long hard battle. Junie and Mama on the couch, cheek-to-cheek at Diana's house on Beachwood. Mama at the table holding maracas wearing a sombrero, May 2005. A group picture of all of us in her room, Junie, Dolores, Diana, Jimmy, and me. Group pictures of all of us, with cousins, many babies, lots of friends, Mama's funeral, June 2005.

They're right there, scattered all over the floor, and I'm on the floor surrounded with them. A picture of me with primos Albert and Ponchie last October, standing in front of Dolores' house after my brother Junie's funeral. I'm smiling, trying to be strong, dying inside.

Still pouring outside, heavy raindrops ping the old wall-heater. I take a deep breath, lay flat on the floor, press my face gently to the pictures, close my eyes.

"Mine…all mine," I say tearfully.

Below:
Sarabia, Grandma Socorro, Daddy

Top: Gena, Diana, and Inez, Tijuana 1971

Bottom: Cousin Eva and me

Picture Books (2002)

"Stop hitting your sister! Don't slam the door!" Mama yells from the kitchen as I chase my sister Lola through the living room and out the door many years ago. Her voice and the moment, still as clear as the delicious aroma of fideo and chopped hotdogs simmering on the stove. Ours was a poor house, but full of life.

I pulled the box of family albums, most from times growing up in Merced. Mama had stacks of old photo albums. Pictures tell a story, as the song goes. One album in particular, was filled with yellowed obituary clippings from the Merced Sun-Star and copies of the brochures handed out at the funeral. A unique record of family deaths, taped next to pictures of family members lying in open caskets. We called this album, Mama's Death Book.

As kids, we found this photo album weirdly fascinating, and asked lots of questions about relatives we never knew. As we got older though, the people lying in those caskets, became too familiar. When my father and brother showed up in the book, that was too close. "Mama, you really shouldn't take pictures of them in their caskets, it looks creepy." "No Mijo, this is where I honor their memory," she answered sincerely. "Ay Mama," I said shaking my head, "Hope I never end up in this book."

In another photo album, a recent picture of the family reunion 1997. We're out in the country at my cousin Arturo's house off Snelling Way in Merced. At this reunion, older cousins Natalia and Lupita are sitting with their plates of food, grubbing heartily. Their children, and their children's children, all in folding chairs sitting next to them. Large parts of the family were sectioned off all over the big lot. Alonzos, Avinas, Saldanas, Cervantes, Marianos. I yell at

Tio Boogie, Daddy, baby Junie

cousin Natalia to smile for the camera. She looks up, food dribbling down her cheek, pleads with me not to take it. "Travieso!" she says laughing.

Cousin Natalia died in 1998 of diabetes, a year later. Her daughter Lulu told me recently she'd found a stack of La Pina flour sacks saved by her mother in a trunk for years. For Lulu, an expert quilter, putting it together was a labor of love. She calls it her 'tortilla quilt." Cousin Lupita died the following year of the same illness.

There's an old black and white photo 1959, of my tios standing next to my grandfather's house behind the Merced Fairgrounds. Tios Charlie and Boogie crouched rackishly on one knee in front, and Tios Mike, Frankie, and Joe, standing in back. It was the day of my cousin Josephine's funeral.

There's another picture taken forty years later after my brother Benjie's funeral. Tia Ofelia, youngest of the girls, full of energy and life, sits next to Mama, Tios Boogie, Charlie, and Frank, outside the housing projects on 7th street. Missing from this picture, are Tias Lupe and Dela, and Tios Mike and Joe. Tia Ofelia died shortly after the picture was taken. Cancer came suddenly, took her quickly.

There's an old picture of Lola and Benjie, born the same day, a year apart. Birthday parties always shared. They're about ten and nine years old, wearing silly paper hats, about to cut the cake. It's a large cake with a carousel and tiny flags waving. Daddy's holding baby brother Jimmy right behind them. Benjie died of a heart attack a few years ago. Every September for years, birthday cakes still had both their names.

Dolores races past the fence, through the back door, then cuts through the kitchen. I catch up to her, yank her pigtails. We're laughing and squealing, running circles around Mama's legs. Mama stomps her feet and bangs the big spoon against the olla on the stove. "Ay dios mio! Don't make me get the belt!" she scolds. Sights and sounds bounce off the walls, ring softly. I put the photo album down, look into Mama's tired eyes and smile.

Here's a great photo of Tio Boogie right after a boxing match, a towel draped over his shoulders. The boxing gloves are off, but his hands are still taped, as he shakes hands with Daddy, who's holding onto baby Junie with his other hand. This is my favorite picture of them. They're both looking directly into the camera, young, smiling, and with full heads of hair. Daddy's no doubt, congratulating Tio Boogie for winning the fight.

These pictures take me home, when I'm not home. That warm, safe place where holidays and parties are festive, embraces constant. If I stare long enough, I hear the kids racing through the house, the smell of fresh made tortillas, Perez Prado on the record-player, Tio Boogie dancing the mambo, and Daddy coming home from the asparagus fields, black from dust and sweat, shaking his boots on the porch.

Pulled out a picture from 1948, and set it on the table. Mama's standing in front of grandpa's house on 11th street. I recognize the giant nopales in the background. She's holding baby Junie, who squeals happily to the camera. Mama looks so sad and serious. Her hair is combed high up, in that familiar way with the big bun in front. Her arm is raised, shading the sun from her eyes. I see all our faces in her eyes. She's wearing a dark, wrinkled suit with a skirt, with bobby-sox and dusty shoes. A rare dress-up day. Probably taken after a funeral.

Standing: Tio Frank, Tio Charlie
Sitting: Tio Boogie, Mama, Tia Ofelia

THE REASON FOR (2005)

This morning, the room emptier than usual, the summer heat fell behind a cold, cloudy sky. Not bone-chilling, not yet. Should be glad I can feel it. Daddy and my brothers can't. Mama can't. Many friends, who fell way too early, can't. Accidents, suicides, health, age, take a number, form a line.

*The house on K Street
left to right/standing: Tia Lupe, Tio Frank,
Tio Joe, Tio Boogie
sitting: Mama, Tio Charlie*

Don't know what it is about today. The air so thick, the music playing mournful sax from the sixties, real low, just enough. In a bar, drinking alone, the world dying at my feet.

There was a moment earlier, a stop at the dentist. Maybe that's what did it. I mentioned seeing him outside last week. "Thought you were taller," I said, "of course, I'm always tilted, looking up." He laughed.

He told me something about his sick mother, and I, in turn, talked a little about mine. I spoke slowly, carefully. Didn't want to say too much. Didn't want to break. "My mother was in hospice a very long time," was all I could say.

At the end, the room packed with relatives, her breathing racing, racing. We held her, raced with her, every breath, until finally, it slowed, and we slowed, slower, slower, then she stopped. My sister tearfully stroked her hair, saying over and over, "it's ok Mama, its ok."

It's not often anymore, although I stop occasionally, and weep privately.

"Hey Mama, remember that time last year when you talked to yourself in the mirror, made us laugh?" "Oh mijo, I was in so much pain, didn't want you to know," she said, "I wanted you to smile, not cry."

"I know Mama, I cried anyway..."

The Family Place

long before
Mama died
she and her sisters,
Adela and Ofelia
bought cemetery plots
side by side
together

back then
thought it was weird
the way they were so obsessed
with this dying place

we had nothing
and yet, for decades
payment for that plot,
without fail
sometimes, she made us
take the money
straight to the cemetery office
when late

now,
our mothers are gone
the emptiness
pain of losing, still too real

i drive home to Merced
Calvary Cemetery
sit at the shade tree,
touch the grass, wipe the dust
carefully, lovingly,
from their pictures

Mama and my tias,
tres hermanas,
Maria, Adela, Ofelia,

they knew,
eventually i'd come
that we'd all come

*Granddaughter Taylor at Mama's funeral,
Calvary Cemetery in Merced 2005*

Old Grey Suitcase

looking for Daddy's letters
again
figured it had to be there,
where i haven't looked, haven't gone
in over thirty years

stuffed my life,
into a small grey suitcase
locked it, then duct-taped around it
at least ten times

wasn't expecting to go back,
maybe never

it was a period of heartache, agony
buried deep in the garage
under decades of junk

didn't want to see it again,
should've burned it

perched strategically on top,
to mark the spot,
my Royal manual typewriter
with the words 'write on'
scratched on the metal cover, 1969

opened the suitcase,
and succumbed to the smell of years,
volumes of stained, yellowed pages
poems, stories, letters
of a pitifully lost, unrecognizable me,
old wounds

searching for Daddy,

piles of dust and paper
fragile threads
of a damaged son,
who lost his father
then closed the door,
too quickly

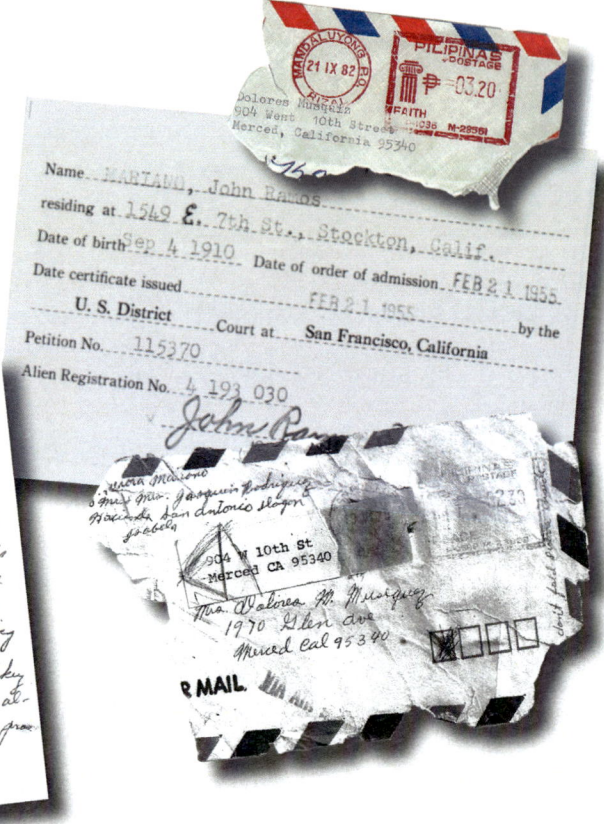

Letter 1

Hi;

We haven't heard from you for so long, we wonder what has happened. Hope everyone is fine, which should put us the same at this time. Thank God. Have written you several letters but you have not answered them. Did Charlie get the two letters and enclosed pictures I sent him? Hope he'll come to Merced for the Holydays. This is another X'mas Aurora & I will not be with you sweetheart, much to our regret. Hope it wouldn't happen again.

Well here we are still in the Phil. It has been raining continuously and hard and our plans and project is terribly slow, which can't be helped. We're doing alright and don't worry about us. Will John and Charlie send me a few used car tools, I need them to fool around on my jeep, we also got us a mini bus for hauling people, we got it as part payment on the money they owe us. I'm missing all the conveniences and good living we are used in the States, and I'm lonely. I miss you all. Tell everyone hello for us, and think of us on your X'mas dinner and all the trimmings. Hi and love to everyone.

Dad.

Letter 2

706 Camacam St.
Santiago, Isabela
Feb. 13, 1979

received your letter here in Santiago aboard
Sweetheart, I could hardly keep the tears
don't know how greatful we are to hear
came at this very moment. I hate to tell
will all feel bad but, with all sincerity I
really happened to me. Yesterday,
Sanitarium & Hospital. I had been
I had a terrible heart attack at that
we again, because I waited too long if
my last check-up. It was almost nine (9) months since I had
could be so careless. Sometimes, I had also other complications that made
matter so worst besides the enlargement of the heart which Doctor
claimed that I was going to anytime. I had athritis and gout my
regular problem in the State. Only this time, I had 11% of Uric
Acid. On top of that, the Doctor claimed, I have also "Diabities" and
"Gland Enlargement." Dolores sweetheart, I was an awful shape and
never felt so bad, and so desperate to live. An examine, I thought that was the end for me.
Other thing, that complic—

have all the ne—

more

is due to the fact that they don't
treatments. Luckily, I had few
been taking which I'm sure to
pills to take and I don't know
dear, this is where you come
Maze Drug Store which
send it as fast as you

that I will have my regular
been, please remember me in your

Naturalization Index

John Ramos Mariano, "California, Northern U.S. District Court Naturalization Index, 1852–1989"

Name: John Ramos Mariano
Event Type: Naturalization
Event Date: 1955
Event Place: San Francisco
Age:
Birth Year: 1910
Birth Year (Estimated):
Birthplace:
Affiliate Publication Title:
Affiliate Publication Number:
Affiliate Film Number:
Digital Folder Number:
Image Number:

Piece Work — Slices of Life

Plastic Flowers (2006)

The sad thing about getting older, as most people know, is you start attending more funerals. Then again, you can make up a rule and refuse to go to these stark reminders of losses, especially those that hit hard. If you're a sensitive, caring soul like me though, then that's a tough sell. I get this all-feeling, all-caring heart from my mother, I'm sure of it. Another thing about funerals, is if you no longer live in the town where you were born, then trips down the 99 freeway are frequent.

This isn't about another funeral thoughy, it's about the cemetery where most of these funerals take place. Calvary Cemetery is at the corner of Child's Avenue and Martin Luther King Boulevard in Merced. It's where most of my family and friends on these solemn occasions, end up. The losses these days take a toll, and I find myself more and more, staring beyond the cyclone fence that encloses the cemetery to the side facing Hoffman Lane.

We lived in so many houses in Merced, it's a wonder I can keep track. It was never one house, because we were always moving. There was the house on 12th street, the house on McGregor, the house on Cone Avenue, the house on Olive Avenue, the house at 1231 K, Beachwood Drive, and many others. Each house had its own place and story.

Tio Boogie and Mama at Grandma Socorro's grave, Calvary Cemetery, 1949

The house on Hoffman was memorable for a few reasons. When I was a kid, it was a short, dirt-gravel road that deadended into a poorman's cul-de-sac. Potholes, mud, pieces of wood and glass were all part of the road. There were only about a dozen houses and all of them were in bad shape. The one at very end with the most potholes in front of it, was Mama's house. Daddy lived across the street in a smaller, flat-roofed house.

From the time I could comprehend clearly, my mother and father never lived in the same house, and there was always a great distance between the houses. They didn't fight or threaten or anything like that. It was more of a silent agreement to get along for the sake of us kids. Every one of us, absolutely adored my father, it was no contest. The houses on Hoffman was the only time in our lives that Daddy and Mama lived so close. It was almost like living together.

Perhaps the most significant reason, aside from having everyone together in one spot, was that we lived right next to Calvary Cemetery. When we were kids, a cyclone fence and dirt field was all that separated the cemetery from the house. All the new burials were near our side of the cemetery. The bigger headstones and tombs were on the old side.

Living right next to the cemetery wasn't really that scary. You'd think we'd get caught up in all the ghost talk and be afraid to go out at night, or hear noised, but it wasn't anything like that. For me, the people on that side of the fence were our neighbors. Real quiet, but still neighbors. We also knew to respect the dead. Not being afraid of the cemetery was convenient too, because it was directly between us and going into town, so it was our shortcut. All we had to do was climb the fence and cut right down the middle to Child's Avenue, which was also a hop skip from the Merced Fairgrounds.

During the work day when the caretakers were out, it was off limits, but when they left then this big area turned into our own personal park to play in. This was mostly during early evenings when it was still light. Nighttime playing took a while to get used. Respecting the dead was one thing, but when you turn off the lights, a whole different ballgame. I had to force myself to walk through a few times at night alone, until it didn't bother me too much. Sort of like a rite of passage to facing fear.

I used to get a kick out of telling people directions to our house. "Go down J Street (now MLK), hang a right on Hoffman, and it's right behind Calvary Cemetery."

"You live behind the cemetery?" they'd shriek, "That must be scary." We just laughed. Little did they know, for most of us, particularly my sister Dolores and I, the cemetery was our playground. The best game to play in the cemetery was hide and seek, especially on the side that had headstones and tombs. We were always trying to scare each other out there. When cousins or other kids came to visit, right away we'd steer the games toward the cemetery.

One time my friend Raymond came over and when it got dark, we talked him into playing out there. They idea of playing in the cemetery at night didn't exactly sit too well, but being called chicken by a girl, was too much to take. When we got out there, we picked Raymond to count first. "One...two...three..." Dolores, Benjie, and I, scattered different directions. I leaped over a dozen headstones then bee-lined to the tombs. We could barely hear Raymond finishing his count. "Seven...eight...nine...ten. Ready or not, here I come!"

He ran back and forth, humming some song loudly to keep from getting scared, then tripped over an uneven section and fell right where Dolores was hiding. "Hah! Caught you. One down," Raymond yelled. Dolores tagged along with him while he searched for Benjie and I. Benjie laid flat as a board on his back across a plot like a dead person, so when Raymond and Dolores got close, he just sat up suddenly and yelled.

"Boo!"

"Damn it Benjie, you almost gave me a heart attack!" cried Raymond. Dolores and Benjie are cracking up, rolling on the grass. "C'mon, help me find Charlie."

Near the back section there was a tomb I could climb up the side and hide on top. I laid real still, and waited for Raymond. By then, Dolores and Benjie had slipped away from Raymond and left him walking by himself. "Alright Charlie, I give up. Come out now, you win," cried Raymond.

I held my breath until he got right beneath me, then at the last second, pounced on him. "Yaaahhhaaarrrgh!" I screamed. Benjie and Dolores popped out from behind a tomb at the same time yelling too. We rolled on the grass screaming, and laughing. Raymond was angry as hell.

"Damn you guys, you made me pee my pants!" Then he started laughing too.

One night at home, Dolores and I saw Mama making a plastic flower arrangement in the kitchen. "Who's that for Mama?" I asked.

"This is for Emilia's daughter's party at the Woman's Club," she said, "They're paying me to make a few arrangements. In our family, it was no secret we needed money. Most of our lives we were on welfare. Being hungry and poor, was normal. Dolores and I walked outside thinking the same thing. We knew where there were flowers, tons of flowers.

People would bring flowers all the time to the cemetery. They'd stay on the headstones for a couple of days, then the workers would gather them all up and trash them. There was a big pile just outside the fence. We walked over to the pile and saw they'd mixed the flowers with a lot of wet landscaping, so we thought about it for two seconds, then climbed over the fence and started gathering up plastic flowers from the headstones. We only picked the best, fanciest flowers.

When both our arms were full, we helped each other across the fence, then walked back to the house and into the kitchen. Mama looked up at us in shock. "Ay dios mio, where did you get those?" she scolded. We thought she'd be pleased, and now it looked like we were in big trouble. Then slowly, her expression softened from shock, to anger, to practical. "Ay, you kids," she said shaking head, "Bring them over by the sink so I can wash them."

We weren't sure how much Mama made from those flowers, but it became a small source of income. It was our job now, to gather the plastic flowers when needed. We wouldn't get them every night, and never from the same area. We tried to respect the dead, even though what we were doing was sort of immoral. We rationalized it by saying it was something useful, and needed. Besides, by now the dead people in our playground were our friends, and were helping us.

We didn't go every night, sometimes we'd wait weeks or a month, then Mama would say out of the blue, "I need to make some flowers." We knew right away it was time to go to work. People would come over and find dozens of flower arrangements, washed and hanging on strings drying. Mama rigged a couple line straight across the kitchen and part of the living room. The house looked and smelled like a funeral parlor of plastic flowers. Mama really got into the creative production of the arrangements too, having so many choices to make each one look fantastic. It was a happy time.

I've always felt there's something a little tacky about our family that goes beyond normal. Not in a negative sense though. Even after I moved away and now make a decent living, nothing's changed. Like when buying a gift for my mother, I'd sometimes go for the low-brow stuff, because

Mama holding baby Benjie

I knew how much she liked to laugh. One time had an industrial sized box of toilet paper nicely gift-wrapped, with a tag on it that read, For the whole family. Another time I cracked her up with a singing James Brown doll that would sing "I Feel Good," and break out with a few moves. On my next visit home, she'd have James high on the shelf in the front room, a place of honor.

At work one day a woman asked me, "Why do you buy your family things like that?"

"Because I know my family," I answered, "We're tacky, and proud of it. In fact, the tackier, the better." Like velvet-framed pictures of JFK and Elvis, or big, gaudy pictures of the Virgin Mary. There was something warm and personal about that part of us, a bond that hits home.

I watched as they lowered Mama into the hole one hot summer day in June. One by one, family and friends stepped across to drop handfuls of dirt. The grief and sadness in the air was heavy. I gazed momentarily passed them to the row of houses on Hoffman Lane. The empty field was filled-in with fresh burial plots and headstones. It was much closer now, practically on the doorstep of our old house. It's strange, but it felt like we were bringing Mama home.

A month later, my sister Dolores calls me on the phone to tell me the stone was finally placed at the plot, they only had to finish setting the picture in it. "When it's done, come to Merced, and you and I can buy some fresh flowers and go visit her." I could hear her crying as she told me this. Things about Mama are still too hard to accept.

I thought about what she'd just said about the flowers. "No," I said, "We'll get her plastic flowers."

"Plastic?" she says shocked, "That's tacky."

"Think about it," I told her.

She went silent a moment, then I could hear her laughing. "Yeah, you're right, Mama would prefer plastic flowers."

Dolores & Daddy at the Flea Market on Child's Avenue, Merced, CA

Special Thanks & Acknowledgement

To the Filipino-American farmers 'Manongs' of Merced County (1960-1975)

Tony Dumpit, Primo Hullana, Christo Hidalgo, Mel Acosta, Al Balanon & John R. Mariano

    I wrote this book to honor my father, but in reality, it is to honor fathers everywhere of all cultures, who have shaped and touched our lives deeply. To the farmers, farmworkers and families of the great Central Valley who toiled, sacrificed, and cultivated the fields and dreams of our lives, this book is for you.

Photo Credit, Art & Sources:

Merced County Historical Society Museum Archives – Special thanks to Herb Wood & Sarah Lin for valuable assistance obtaining historical photos of Merced.

UC Merced County Cooperative Extension – Various fruit box labels art (Agricultural & Natural Resource), special thanks Maxwell Norton, Scott Scoto Family.

Label Art Book, Dover Pictura – Various box label art

San Joaquin County Historical Society & Museum (Lodi) – Photos: Filipino worker at asparagus sled in field, asparagus knife image, tomato picking crew (1947) image, man pruning apricot trees, Japanese man pruning grapes. Special thanks David Stuart, Julie Blood, and Leigh Johnsen

San Francisco History Center, SF Public Library – 3 Photos SF Farmers' Market Alemany

California State Archives (Sacramento) – Historical research

Sacramento Genealogical Society (Root Cellar) – Family history research

KVIE/DVD Sacramento, CA – Excerpts from Channel 6 video, 'Little Manila, Filipinos in America's Heartland.'

Bright's Museum/Nursery (LeGrand, CA) – Courtesy of Bright Family – various photos

Busa Family Farms/various photos: Tractors, old truck, planter, hotbeds, farm laborers. Special thanks Dennis Busa.

Library of Congress/Russell Lee – 1 Photo: Mexican laborers arriving in Stockton off train.

Reference from book, 'Filipinos of Stockton,' by Dawn Mabalon, FANHS/Stockton Chapter.

FANHS Stockton Chapter – 1 Photo asparagus fieldworkers pg. 28 of 'Filipinos in Stockton.'

Reference book, 'If You Want Know What We Are,' A Carlos Bulosan Reader

Reference book, 'Voices, A Filipino American Oral History,' by Filipino Oral History Project, Inc.

Stephanie Morimoto (Talking Food/website) – Research guidance to original SF Farmer's Market (Alemany).

Filipino American National Historical Society FANHS/Merced Chapter:

Many thanks to FANHS Chapter in Merced for graciously inviting me into their Christmas luncheon to gather information for this book, in particular Bob Luna and Lourdes Clesson Dumpit.

Further Information research gathered from the book Talk Story, Anthology of Stories by Filipino Americans of the Central Valley of California, published by FANHS Merced Chapter. Other references from this book:

Also from Talk Story: Estella Campion Paculba – Reference about Merced County farming, The Alipio & Alice Paculba Family.

Published letter in Talk Story – 'My Mentor, My Hero: John Ramos Mariano' by C.Mariano.

Bob Luna – Original contact in Merced that first published my letter in FANHS Central Valley newsletter, then again in Talk Story. Bob was instrumental in connecting me to other FANHS members in Merced. Great appreciation and gratitude.

Filipino American National Historical Society FANHS/Sacramento Chapter:

Special thanks FANHS members for inviting me into their meeting, and allowing me to research and ask questions.

Jay Paular – Great appreciation and special thanks to SacBroJay for connecting me to FANHS

Photo Credit, Art & Sources:

Sacramento chapter, and for inviting me into his mother's home. Jay also helped provide his mother Eleanor's Pancit & Chicken Adobo recipes in this book. Finally, for introducing me to his auntie Anita Navalta Bautista of FANHS/Stockton Chapter.

Filipino American National Historical Society FANHS/Stockton Chapter:

Anita Navalta Bautista – My fellow writer and confidante, who was not only a valuable historical resource, but dear friend.

Mel LaGasca – Thanks to Mel for assistance opening doors during critical historical research in Stockton, and for pointing me in the right direction.

Augustine 'Tio Boogie' Alonzo – Family history research, and photo identifications.

Tia Molly 'Pettit' Alonzo – 1 photo, L&G Barnes Circus group (1933), family history, but most of all, heartfelt gratitude for putting up with my annoying phone calls to Fresno.

Dolores Mariano – Various selected photos.

Jasmin Mariano – Various photos including: Hwy 99 sign (view from Gerard Ave), old tractors & trucks, workshop, from Bright's Museum in LeGrand,CA. Photo of Shaffer Bridge in Winton,CA) & Bear Creek & Black Rascal road signs.

Diana Mariano – Photo research assistance & photo of Merced Theater at night

Melina Aguilar – Historical documentation research on my father (her grandpa).

Jimmy Mariano – Photo used at end, Lola & Daddy, Merced Flea Market

Nash Musquiz Jr. – Photo used in Daddy's Skin.

Adelita Woodley – Photo of Mama, Tia Dela, and Tia Lupe, standing as teens

Isabel Avina – Cousin Lulu, who gave me full access to her personal photo collection.

Rudy Cuellar – Photo of Rolo's bus, used in Bus Stop.

Robert Lee Haycock – Photo of Golden Gate bridge in fog & photo view from SF Bay Bridge used in Magic Kingdom.

Trent Harger – Rocker Foto in Oaxaca, Mexico, used in Tortillas an Bread.

Francisco Dominguez – 1 photo, Chavez Funeral in Delano,CA 1994, 'The Eagle Transcends' copyright Francisco Dominguez.

Lourdes Dumpit Clesson & Dumpit family – 3 photos of old SF Farmer's Market (Alemany), circa 1960, used in Magic Kingdom

Josie Cervantes – For quote at beginning of Snake Lady.

Laura Llano – Cactus image used in Cactus House.

Caltrafficsigns.com – Various Hwy 99 signs, special thanks to Brian & Karen Smith

AARoads – Various road signs

Friends of the River – Photographer Mike Osborn for 3 photos of Merced River used in Driving Down the Santa Fe & Heartland. Special thanks, Ron Stork.

Emilio Soltero – 1 photo of old truck, Merced truck image used in In the Mix.

Paul Martzen – Photo of Shaffer Bridge.

Mareia de Socorro, Co-Madres Artistas de Sacra. Artwork, The Curtain Rises on Mole used in poem Footprints.

CREDITS & SOURCES

All other photos used in this book are from my personal family collection.

Song of the San Joaquin (Modesto, California) – Selected poems first published in SSJ, reprinted: Fields and Dreams, Alligator Hands, Farmer's Market, Father's Day, Broken Home, Alzheimer's, Farming, The 99, Purple People Eater, Footprints, The House on 12th, Shoes, Where Old Tractors Go to Die, Overplayed, The Artist, Heartland

Special thanks to Cleo Griffith/ Song of the San Joaquin, for unwavering faith, but most of all sincere friendship.

Indiana State University – This Winter, first published in Indiana State Review.
Escritores del Nuevo Sol - Sincere thanks to the best writer's group in Sacramento, for support and friendship.

Front Cover Design – Janet Mason, ideas by design
Back Cover Design - Janet Mason, ideas by design
Interior Design and Layout – Janet Mason, ideas by design
On-call Photoshop Assistance – Rudy Cuellar
Proofing – Andrea Cortez, Joaquin Galvan, Emilio Soltero
For friendship, insightful wisdom, moral compass- Joaquin D. Galvan

Recipes:
(Jay Paular's mother)
Chicken Adobo Recipe – by Eleanor Engkabo Paular
Pancit Recipe – by Eleanor Engkabo Paular

As always, sincere love and appreciation for my family. I'm nothing without them.

Tio Frank Alonzo
April 20, 1922 - April 9, 2013

Chicken Adobo

By Eleanor Engkabo Paular

Ingredients:

1 - 2½ lb whole chicken or 8 - 10 thighs

2 tblspn finely chopped garlic

½ cup white vinegar

¼ cup soy sauce

2 bay leaves

1½ tspn salt

¾ tspn black pepper (or black peppercorns)

boiling water

2 tblspn oil

1. Clean chicken, cut into 2 inch pieces
2. Combine chicken, vinegar, and seasonings
3. Add enough boiling water to barely cover chicken; cover, and simmer until chicken is tender and water has evaporated
4. Add the oil and fry chicken until brown, serve over rice

Some may not want to fry at step 4, boiling only is also fine.

PANCIT RECIPE   *(8 servings)*

By Eleanor Engkabo Paular

Ingredients:

1 lb. pork or chicken, finely chopped

8 oz. finely cut egg noodles

3 ½ tsp. salt

⅛ tsp. black pepper

8 cups boiling water

⅓ cup finely chopped onion

1 clove garlic

2 cups sliced tomatoes

1 ½ tbl fat

Garnish:

¼ finely chopped peanuts

2 fried eggs, cut into shreds

6 slices lemon

¼ cup finely chopped green onion

Cover noodles with boiling water, add 1 ½ tsp salt, boil until noodles are soft.
Drain, wash with cold water and drain again.

Mash garlic, fry in 1 tbl fat. When brown, discard it and fry onion until partially soft, add pork or chicken and ¼ cup water, simmer till meat is tender. Add tomatoes, 1½ salt, simmer until tomatoes are cooked.
Pour boiling water over noodles to reheat them, drain, and mix with the meat and vegetables.
Garnish the dish with peanuts, egg strips, lemon slices, and the green onions.
Add sliced shitaki mushrooms to the vegetables to kick up the flavor.

(another version: add sliced cabbage to the vegetables)